NEW LIVES FOR

BY THE SAME AUTHOR:

FORGOTTEN SKIES

INDIAN SUMMER

FLAME OF THE FOREST AND OTHER POEMS

MERCHANT IN A MIRROR

THE FRIENDLY FIRM

With J. G. Speer

SAHIBS AND SAHDUS

NEW LIVES FOR OLD:

The Story of the Cheshire Homes

by

WILFRID RUSSELL

with a foreword by

H.R.H. THE DUKE OF EDINBURGH

and a note by

GROUP CAPTAIN LEONARD CHESHIRE
V.C., D.S.O., D.F.C.

LONDON
VICTOR GOLLANCZ LTD
1980

First published 1963
This revised edition published 1980

ISBN 0 575 02807 6

NOTE

All royalties earned by the sale of this book will go to the Cheshire Foundation.

Printed in Great Britain at
The Camelot Press Ltd, Southampton

This book is dedicated to the memory of Primrose Cheshire, who sustained her son with love and understanding and who died at Laundry Cottage, Liss, on the 16th of March, 1962.

FOREWORD
BY H.R.H. THE DUKE OF EDINBURGH

The history of the treatment of the sick and the disabled is illuminated by the flashing humanity of a handful of reformers and innovators. Leonard Cheshire joins that select group for the world-wide network of homes for the incurably sick which he has managed to establish in the face of every kind of difficulty and discouragement.

People are never likely to get to know a problem or to appreciate its importance unless it affects them personally. The problem of the incurably sick tends to be hidden from the public view and so to many people it doesn't exist. This book displays all the difficulties and unthinking—not deliberately thoughtless—inhumanity which these people have to face as they share the gift of life with their more fortunate neighbours. For a great many the burden must have been hardly tolerable until they found the sustaining comfort and simple encouragement of a Cheshire Home.

This is the story of one of the greatest acts of humanity in our time.

Philip

29th January, 1963

NOTE
BY GROUP CAPTAIN CHESHIRE

WILFRID RUSSELL CAME to our help in India at a time when we badly needed someone who had just the qualities and just the influence that he had. He has continued helping more and more ever since. To me, as I write this Foreword, he symbolizes all those people who at different times since the beginning of the story which he recounts have appeared out of the blue, as he did, to help the patients. Many of them have done whatever it was that needed doing without asking for acknowledgement or recognition and then continued on their way, to be lost from sight, though not from memory. It is these above all to whom my thoughts turn, since I often have no means of expressing my appreciation to them in person; and their example which has inspired and strengthened me. I know only too well that, when the veil that stands between us and eternity has fallen, there are many who now appear to be first in works of charity who will then be found to be last, and many last who will then be first.

This book has been written in order to make better known the needs of those who are chronically sick or disabled, and to emphasize how much they can contribute to the good of the world if only given the chance. But it will also, I hope, give an insight into some of the pitfalls which we ourselves have met—and at times fallen into—and so perhaps be of some use to others who may be setting out along similar paths. For myself, it has helped me both to remember the debt of gratitude which I owe to a great many people, and to be more aware of the need that the modern world has of goodwill if it is not to disintegrate. In my own opinion the great mission of those who suffer and are in want is to draw out the inherent goodwill that is in all of us, and so to make us forget ourselves and draw closer one to another in our common journey through life.

LEONARD CHESHIRE

CONTENTS

LIST OF ILLUSTRATIONS

(*between pages 128 and 129*)

The Leonard Cheshire Foundation United Kingdom

The Leonard Cheshire Foundation International

FRANCE
PAIN
ROCCO
SUDAN
ETHIOPIA
NIGERIA
UGANDA
KENYA
ZAMBIA
SOUTH AFRICA
SEYCHELLES
MAURITIUS
INDIA
SRI LANKA
BANGLADESH
THAILAND
HONG KONG
PHILIPPINES
MALAYSIA
SINGAPORE
INDONESIA
PAPUA NEW GUINEA

CHAPTER ONE

THE PROBLEM

"SO THE SIZE of the problem isn't really known?"

We were sitting in the drawing-room of my house in London. I had been connected with the Cheshire Homes in England and abroad for six years—since 1956, in fact; for a considerable number of them I had been a Trustee of the organization, which was called the Cheshire Foundation Homes for the Sick; and I had seen and known many disabled people with chronic, incurable diseases. But, talking to Cherry Morris, I realized for the first time that beneath our work was a bedrock of ignorance—ignorance of the basic facts, ignorance of the number of chronic sick in the modern world.

Cherry had been with the Homes almost from the beginning. Before that she had been for many years senior almoner of the National Hospital for Nervous Diseases, and she has always been the source of our technical knowledge, one of our principal contacts with the disabilities and diseases of the members of our growing family.

"I don't think we really know any more about how big the problem is than we did when the Health Service first started," she replied.

She went on talking quietly, telling me things I already knew, but had paid little attention to in the day-by-day affairs of the Cheshire Homes.

As she spoke on into the night in her gentle voice, with its undertones of humour and compassion, I began to see the terrifying paradox at the heart of the matter—the existence in our midst of people, many of them young, who have been struck down by incurable diseases. Their lives are being prolonged by drugs, iron lungs, costly appliances of great ingenuity—but prolonged for what? If they are young, at worst to become increasingly a drag on their parents, whose old age looms ever nearer; at best to find a bed in what is professionally called a geriatric ward in a hospital, and is less politely, but more descriptively, referred to as a senile ward.

"What has saddened me," Cherry continued, "is that so far little has been done in any imaginative way to help these people. Almost everywhere material conditions have altered out of all knowledge, yet for the active-minded of any age life in a chronic ward or in Part Three accommodation is still all too often a living death. People are 'existing'—not living—so much longer than they used to, so that in any public institution the very old and the senile swamp everyone else. The authorities persist in regarding this as a small problem, but are they right? In numbers, perhaps, yes, although I think it is fair to doubt even this; in terms of human suffering, emphatically no."

Before the war, although almost nothing had been known of this extraordinary problem, most almoners in the voluntary system had had an inkling of its existence; they suspected that there were in this country many human beings, often young and vital, who had become completely disabled, so that life as they had known it had come to a full-stop. In such cases the limbs are paralysed or become uncontrollable, yet the mind remains as active as before, or may even increase in power. These diseases—disseminated and multiple sclerosis, rheumatoid arthritis, muscular distrophy, and others—strike at the middle-aged as well as the young. The sight of a young man with an incurable disease passing his life away in a senile ward, surrounded by the dying, is so dramatic that it sometimes obscures a situation which concerns men and women of all ages.

True, the problem has changed since the end of the war, since the coming of the National Health Service and the emergence of an affluent society. In 1946 the situation was grim. Here, for instance, is Sir Ernest Rock Carling, speaking at the annual general meeting of the Institute of Almoners in that year:

"Primitive man had a simple way of dealing with his chronic sick. He eliminated them! But is mankind today very much better? We still eliminate a great many by leaving them to live a long-drawn-out death in institutions far removed from everyday life."

So it has remained. In many countries there is today this attitude to deformity of mind or body. The disabled member of the family, often a child, is kept hidden away at the back of the mud hut where the neighbours cannot see the family's disgrace. Is it possible that this is sometimes the case in our own green and pleasant land, and may this be one of the reasons why the size of the problem is not known?

Sir Ernest Rock Carling went on to describe what he called the shadows of a dark picture, the type of buildings in which chronic sick people without means of their own were housed. His description coincides exactly with everything that the word "senile" has always conjured up in my mind.

"Some of these buildings date back to 1837–47, with stone floors, narrow staircases, windows set high up in the walls, dingy brown decorations, and sometimes even inadequate water supplies and lavatory accommodation."

He could, he said, take any doubter the next day and show him half-a-dozen places where these conditions existed.

Outwardly, by 1962, the situation had been transformed. In February of that year I was taken round several geriatric wards in a large North London Hospital. The workhouse atmosphere was wholly absent, and I wondered suddenly whether it had all been swept away by the National Health Service, whether much of what I had been told was exaggerated.

A doctor and two almoners took me round these wards. I spoke to several of the old people. It was an uphill struggle. There was so little to talk about. None of those I talked to had been out of the ward and into the narrow strips of open air and lawn between the ward buildings since they had been there, not even in summer. There was a TV set at the end of the ward, but it didn't look as if it was ever turned on. The spick-and-span appearance of the ward, the bright colour of the walls—no sign of that awful brown Sir Ernest Rock Carling had talked about—the obviously efficient nursing, none of this could hide for long the lack of life in the rows of quiet, neat-looking old people in the beds. And I realized that the problem had changed its nature but was still with us, urgent, baleful, immense.

The doctor who took me round admitted that the inevitable routine, the lack of visitors, the absence of a home atmosphere, which a hospital cannot be expected to create—especially a State hospital—all combine to produce a vacuum of the spirit in which the tiny flame of happiness in these old people seems to snuff out. There was no sign of life in those bright and airy wards.

It so happened there had been no young chronic sick patients in any of the wards we visited, but I was brought face to face with this problem immediately we came out into the roadway joining the hospital blocks. The doctor turned to me and said:

"You know how hard we have been trying to find a bed in a Cheshire Home for one of my patients with multiple sclerosis."

I remembered that he had spoken often about this young woman, whose active life had been tragically and, as always, unexpectedly cut short by the onset of this incurable disease.

"Well, we've managed at last to get her into a holiday bed at St. Bridget's, but only for a month. When that's up, if we haven't been able to find a permanent bed for her in some other Cheshire Home, she will have to come in here."

Thus it was that, for the first time in the six years I had been connected with these Homes, I grasped something of the reality of the situation. There were at that moment thirty-five Cheshire Homes in England, Scotland, Ireland and Wales. Our largely amateur organization is never up to date with statistics, for there are always so many more urgent tasks on hand than calling for paper returns; so we are never certain at any one time how many patients there are in all the Homes. But so far as we knew there were at that time about seven hundred Cheshire beds for the whole of the United Kingdom. We know that every Home has a long waiting-list, and applications are coming in at the rate of one a day to our little head office in Market Mews in the heart of London. And here was someone real, not just a name in a letter, and ten yards away through the swing doors was that lifeless hothouse where all the skill of nursing and of modern medicine was deployed on decaying bodies. Into that atmosphere would go the youthful spirit of a woman in the prime of life—unless the Cheshire Homes could save her.

How infinitely preferable, it seemed to me, was the kind of care she would get in one of the Homes, even though the skilled hospital nursing would be replaced by amateur care in an amateur situation, and the streamlined, functional buildings by one of the tumble-down houses that so often come our way. For the hospital would always be an institution, whereas the Cheshire Home would be a home in the full sense of the word. This is sometimes difficult for professional social workers to appreciate—and how can you blame them? You can only understand these things if you have seen them happen.

I was anxious to find out more about the size of the problem, at any rate in England. One almoner I saw who was particularly interested in the young chronic sick said that she had been to the Ministry of Health, but that nobody there had been able to produce any figures. On the contrary, they had told her that it was the almoners who should be able to provide the Ministry with figures; could she provide some for a start?

I decided to call on a man called Farrell. He had studied architecture before the war, but there had been no time to qualify before he found himself in the R.A.F. In due course he joined a night fighter squadron; in due course he won his D.F.C. At the end of the war he had decided on medicine. He slogged away for the necessary years, qualified, settled down in partnership at Crawley in Sussex, married a beautiful girl, and had two sons. Then in 1956 he got multiple sclerosis. It seemed that not only his life but his wife's was over, and perhaps his children's lives too, almost before they had begun.

I drove down from London, and somewhere on the borders of Surrey and East Sussex lost my way. The lady at the village shop knew all about it.

"Oh, yes, the Cheshire Home at Heatherley. Let's come outside on the road, and I'll show you how to get there." Then followed a clear description of a cross-country journey of several miles. "It's a wonderful place, and they're building a new wing already—they haven't been open a year."

It was indeed a wonderful place, as I discovered when I was shown round it, after my talk with Ginger Farrell.

He was sitting in the morning room off the main hall. He was in his wheel-chair, the morning paper on his knees. This surprised me, because the last time I had seen him he couldn't read—I think because his head used to shake so much, and he couldn't turn over the pages of a book. After he had introduced me to the two young girls in the room, also in wheel-chairs, a nurse came in and pushed him to his private room, panelled, and lined with books from floor to ceiling. His squadron crest hung in one corner. There were pictures and flowers, and through the French window a Sussex garden. When he had wheeled himself into position in front of the window, he told me of his operation at the National Hospital in London.

"It's wonderful, I can read now. It's made all the difference."

His voice was much steadier, too, than I remembered. I told him of my sudden realization after six years of working with the Homes that I scarcely knew the elements of the problem, of which he was such a tragic and important victim.

"I don't think anyone really knows the answer. I know a certain amount about my own disease, multiple sclerosis. It's my belief that there are at least fifty thousand cases in the United Kingdom."

I gasped. He didn't seem to know where this figure came from, but when his wife joined us and sat on the edge of the bed behind his wheel-chair she confirmed it. She had been busy with the builders of the new wing, for she was Chairman of this Home, the latest and one of the most remarkable in the chain. She had to keep going out of the room to meet visitors, to talk to the building foreman, to deal with the constant problems that arise in an enterprise of this kind, which is expanding into fresh building before it has even had time to get into the first stride of its new community life. When she could stay with us for an uninterrupted ten minutes she took up the story:

"When we first knew that Ginger had got the disease we naturally tried to find out as much as we could about it. That's certainly the figure."

"Did you find anywhere for him to go at that time?" I asked her.

"We hadn't much money, of course, but we tried desperately to find a bed in a nursing-home. It was almost impossible. The best we could find was in a two-bed room with the most inadequate nursing at ten guineas a week. It was quite awful. And here we have three hundred names on our waiting list for the extra twenty-four beds when the new building is ready."

Before I drove back to London this brave woman showed me round the new wing, which will take twenty-four patients in a variety of rooms, some with four beds, some with two and some with one. The single-storied building is shaped like an L, the arms embracing what will be a rose garden. I asked her a number of questions as we picked our way over tins of paint and lengths of flex. The bill would come to many thousands. It had been raised already from the people of Sussex.

"What are the architect's fees going to come to?"

She looked a little puzzled.

"Why, nothing. The architect has given us the plans and his supervision as his contribution. The builder is on the Committee. He has been wonderful, too."

I drove from Sussex to Hampshire in my search for more information. Le Court. A fine, modern house built on rising ground commanding a view of one of the loveliest valleys in southern England; home of a community of disabled young people, as vital and dynamic as any group to be found in England. I went to see Frank, one of the most dynamic of them all.

He was in his own room when I arrived, a single room with a fine view over the terrace to the garden and the valley below. He was in his new chair, an electric one given to him by his brother, lying almost at full-length. He has osteo- and rheumatoid-arthritis, and has lost the use of both legs. He can only just move one hand, and uses a special piece of wood about twelve inches long to turn over the pages of the many papers and documents he reads. On the specially designed tray fitted to the chair was a collection of papers, pens and pencils, proofs, books and all the things you see on the desk of a writer. This was his desk.

He flicked a tiny lever on the control column to move his chair a fraction to one side, so that I could squeeze an ordinary chair next to him by his bed. There was a tiny hum as the chair obeyed the pressure from his disabled hand.

I had known Frank for several years, ever since I had come back to England from India for good in 1956. He had been editor of the Le Court magazine, *The Cheshire Smile*, almost since it began when the new Le Court was opened in September, 1954. In those days it had been simply the house magazine of Le Court, regarded by many outsiders as just another piece of therapy for the patients. Since I had known him the little mimeographed pamphlet had blossomed into a printed quarterly journal which goes to the four corners of the world. Our friendship had grown out of our meetings over the magazine. But I had never heard his story.

On this afternoon, when I told him I was to write a book about the whole thing, we had a long talk about incurables in contemporary society. He appeared to have as little information about the size of the problem as most other people I had questioned; but he had very definite views about the spiritual side of the matter. He is one of the small group who are constantly working to bring to the world of healthy people the concept of disabled men and women as contributors to society, not exiles from it; as men and women who are not different because they are disabled; as human beings whose minds may become stronger and broader just because they are disabled.

At the age of sixteen, while still at school, he was overtaken by rheumatoid arthritis, which progressed until he was severely incapacitated. Forced to accept the terrible fact that he would spend the rest of his life in that way, he continued to read; the reading became predominantly theological and philosophical. His family looked after him, but he knew this arrangement could not last much longer. He soon made up his mind to find somewhere to live where he would not be a burden to his family and where, if this should be possible, he could continue his theological studies. The almoner at the hospital where he went for treatment knew of his plan, and showed him an article about a pioneering venture for disabled people in Hampshire. She thought it might be a good idea for him to go there for a holiday—he could see whether the place appealed to him as a permanent home. He agreed, and she made all the arrangements. So in June, 1954, he came to the original Le Court.

"You ask me what is the size of the problem, how many people there are in these islands suffering from incurable diseases. I'm afraid I don't know. I wonder if anyone knows, even in the statistical departments of the National Health Service. Obviously it's important to know, but I'm more interested in what can be done for people in my position apart from keeping our broken-down bodies ticking over. It's quite surprising what can be done today to help us in all the activities of daily living, even if medicine can't cure our diseases. What the Health Service hasn't a clue about is how to keep us going as integrated people, how to keep our spirit alive. You see, the rehabilitation teams in this country and in others, especially the U.S.A., have concentrated all their energies on getting the less severely disabled back into circulation as normal citizens in society. In numbers this is the greater problem. But there is this other problem which may be smaller in numbers, but is more intractable. I think the experts have been neglecting what might be done for the severely disabled who must face up to the shattering realization that they can never be cured."

"What is the thing you all need most if you are to feel at all reconciled to your situation?" I asked.

"It's difficult to say, briefly, but I suppose it amounts to four things—to be as independent as possible, to be helped to accept one's dependencies, to have something useful to do, and to feel wanted."

I remembered then something a psychiatrist had said on the occasion when Lord Denning, the Chairman of the Homes, had opened the beautiful new wing of the Bromley Home, St. Cecilia's. It had been a marvellous day, the sun as hot and the sky as blue as in December in Bombay. The psychiatrist, who always seemed to me to speak a lot of sense in his television interviews, was having a public discussion with Ginger Farrell out on the lawn, in front of a large crowd which included half the mayors of Kent. He had explained in this discussion one of the lessons he had learned about what goes on inside the mind of a chronically disabled person, which he had been told by Farrell. He quoted from this doctor-patient:

" 'A patient in one Home I was staying at—he was far more disabled than I was—asked for the paper, which happened to be on a table in the middle of the room. Before I could get my wheel-chair up to the table to take over the paper to my friend, a visitor, who thought she was being given a fine opportunity to help, rushed to the table and took the paper across, beating me easily and making me only too conscious of my dependent state. It was a little thing, but I was bitterly disappointed.' "

Frank and I talked for a long time about this aspect of the problem, and I realized once more how few of us who have been trying to help really can have much idea of how it feels to be sitting in the chair rather than wheeling it.

When I got home that Saturday evening I found, as was so often to happen, that something important, even vital, had turned up at precisely the moment when it was most needed. It came in a bulky envelope from the North-East Metropolitan Regional Hospital Board. I opened the envelope and took out a thick mimeographed report. It was a study, made under the auspices of the Nuffield Foundation, of the patients between the ages of fifteen and fifty-five in the chronic sick wards of hospitals and in local authority accommodation and Homes in the boroughs of North London, including Hackney, Stepney, Bow, Tottenham, Enfield and Edmonton, and stretching out into the countryside to Hertford, Chelmsford, Colchester and Southend. Although the report dealt with only one region, this region was one of the most densely populated, and presumably one of the most representative, in the country. It had come to me through the kindness of the doctor who had taken me round the geriatric wards of one of the hospitals included in the study, and of the Senior Administrative Medical Officer concerned.

The report was the work of Miss Ann Whitaker, an almoner at the National Hospital for Nervous Diseases, supported by a doctor and an influential steering committee, the Chairman of which was Professor Titmuss. It had been begun in February, 1956, the object being primarily to learn and estimate what improvements or differences in care and accommodation were needed for these patients. The aim was also—and, as I read the report, this seemed to me the most important point of all—to distinguish between those who needed skilled medical and nursing care and those needing only care and attention, who were in hospital simply because they had nowhere else to go.

The first thing which struck me about this report was that it had been written by a worker within the National Health Service, but with the financial and advisory assistance of free enterprise. It was a very human document, based on an intelligent and compassionate study of some three hundred cases. It could never have been produced by a Government department. There was, quite rightly and understandably, nothing critical in it of the National Health Service, yet every line seemed to cry out that this particular problem cannot readily be tackled by Government institutions, not even by Government hospitals, for many of the cases interviewed in chronic sick wards did not require the high degree of medical care and attention that was available to them.

The red tape surrounding the patients—inevitable, perhaps, but stifling without doubt—which I had sensed in my own visit to the geriatric wards was confirmed by the author in words meant, I am sure, to be constructive rather than critical.

"The number of services which may be called in to make a contribution at one stage of disability or another speaks in itself of complication: the general practitioner, the general or teaching hospital for diagnosis and treatment at the early and acute stage of illness, the Disablement Resettlement Officer at the Ministry of Labour when disability has set in and special working conditions are necessary, the Ministry of Health for a wheel-chair and/or for a motor chair, the National Assistance Board, the Ministry of National Insurance, the Local Authority Welfare Department, the Medical Officer of Health for district nurse and home help, the Housing Department, the Red Cross or the voluntary society for visits and outings, the National Association for the Paralysed for a holiday."

After listing this formidable number of bodies and people who may be responsible in our Welfare State for looking after an incurably sick person, the report went on to say:

"At present there is no single person or body recognized

as responsible (at any one time) for relating these services to the patients' needs and to each other."

The further I read on, the more certain I became that Miss Whitaker's solution corresponded exactly with the conditions the Cheshire Homes were trying to create. In one chapter she remarked on the similarity between the pattern of life in a chronic sick ward and that in acute wards where everything is subordinated to the needs of acute medicine and its special procedures—the hours of rising and going to bed, visiting times, the absence of organized entertainment, the reduction of personal life to the minimum and the compression of personal belongings into one small locker. All right, perhaps, for the acute case who hopes to get back to a home and to normal living. But for a disabled man or woman, particularly one who is still young, the wards themselves are as unlike an individual home as can be imagined. As the report said in its own stark language, "The rows of beds and cot beds, the prevalence for many hours of the day of night attire, the silence and the slow moving about of the very old, the lack of privacy and of variety are very marked."

What did the author put forward as a solution? On the psychological side she has clearly hit the nail on the head by attributing much of the difficulty to the attitude of all of us—and she does not spare the Health Service itself—to chronic illness. I don't think it would be an exaggeration to say that at any rate in the lay world many of us shrink instinctively from the sight of a bad case of multiple sclerosis, just as people still do in India and Africa from a leper. The uncontrolled shaking of head and hands is always distressing to a healthy person, but often it seems to result in a feeling of revulsion, a feeling that the mind inside the shaking head must be as unstable as the limbs it evidently cannot control. In the opinion of Miss Whitaker and her committee, much could be done to mitigate suffering and even to postpone final breakdown in the home, if there could be a different attitude to chronic illness.

Behind the detached, clinical language of one of her paragraphs there seems to be an indictment of a whole attitude of mind to this problem among professional men. She is writing of the preliminary stage when the disease is suspected by an agonized parent. The young man or woman is taken to hospital for diagnosis. The verdict is pronounced: care at home for a year or two, and then he will have to come into hospital, perhaps for ever.

"We believe that at the general hospital stage, where diagnosis and specific treatment takes place, a far more systematic and intensive provision is needed for the home care of patients, who on discharge are pronounced chronic. Normally there was a lack of medical and social interest in following up these patients. In many cases, although a disabled patient would be provided with a wheel-chair and possibly a medical certificate recommending re-housing, there was little evidence of thought as to how the patient might be helped to live more or less normally for as long as possible."

The report ends with a stirring call to the National Health Service, which, as Miss Whitaker and her committee point out, is surely faced here with a desperate challenge. Her solution is the establishment of residential centres for young chronic sick to be run by the Regional Hospital Boards and local authorities. She urges the grouping of young and middle-aged men and women of active mind in a setting far different from the hospital ward and quite separated from hospital wards themselves, where the routines and medicine inevitably limit the day-to-day activities of patients. Medical and nursing care must be kept in the background, and normal life in the foreground. She is concerned with the correct wheel-chair for the man with the paralysed legs so that he can get out and about to church or the shops or park, with a setting which cares for each person's needs as they arise and which envisages the comings and goings of the disabled between centres of this kind and their own homes for a change and a holiday.

If Government departments and institutions can display individualism to handle what is a problem of individuals, this could be the answer; but is that not a contradiction in terms? *Can* this particular problem be dealt with by administration, by centres, by concentration of effort, however human and understanding the officials administering the centres may be?

The answer to this question lies in the future. What is certain is that the problem is capable of solution psychologically if all the things that Miss Whitaker and her committee could see were necessary are in fact done. I know that this is so because I have seen them being done, even if today it is only for a handful when there are apparently so many knocking at the door.

I have told briefly the stories of two men who have found homes in which they can carry on their lives not only in peaceful surroundings but in situations where they actively influence and strengthen the healthy people with whom they come in contact. A week earlier I had talked with a middle-aged man in Norfolk who had other evidence to contribute. He had been for years in a senile ward at Peterborough Hospital with men and women of seventy and eighty all round him.

"They were just waiting to die," he said.

Theo, as he is known, is now at the new Cheshire Home ten miles outside Norwich. He has rheumatoid arthritis in the hands and feet, so that he cannot walk. He has a wheel-chair. He told me he was fifty-nine and a bachelor. He was oozing cheerfulness.

"I was fit as a flea all my life and fond of sport, football particularly. I was a builders' merchant, mostly in East Anglia. I got this thing when I was fifty, and went into hospital at Peterborough. They were good to me and kept me as long as they could in the medical wards, but when it was clear I couldn't get any better I was moved to the old people's ward."

He said it had been quite awful, through no fault of the hospital. He was surrounded by old people, most of them incontinent.

"The stench was dreadful. I've never smoked so much in my life. And the routine was soulless. They had a TV, but it was nothing like this," and he waved his hand at the TV set in the lovely sitting-room where we were talking. The two-thirty at Hurst Park was just starting, but he had very decently agreed to leave it to talk with me in the bow window looking out over the sweep of lawn down to a beautiful lake. Several kinds of duck were parading on the verge of the lake.

"Here," Theo went on, "there's so much doing I never even have time to read a book, and I like reading. Like betting, too—I've got something on this race."

I said he ought to go back quickly to see the finish. He said not to worry, he had something on two of the later ones.

Then he was off again. "You know how I came here?"

"No."

"Well, I'll tell you. I was in the depths of despair at Peterborough, when one of the nurses came into the ward and said she had seen a programme on TV which was just the thing for me. The Cheshire Homes. So I applied, and here I am. And what's more, I'm going to get better. There was a doctor chap in here the other day who has an arthritis hospital, so he says, somewhere near London, and he thinks he can get me walking again. I'm going there for six weeks quite soon."

I couldn't help thinking how lucky Theo had been to have applied in this part of the country at the very moment when a new Home was starting up. He smiled at me with a red, cheerful face and finished off the conversation:

"You bet I made sure they would keep my place warm for me here."

We wheeled back to the TV set and the next race, amidst the bowls of early daffodils.

The secret of it all appears to lie in the attitude of the healthy rather than in the numbers of the chronic sick—that, at least, seems to me to be the heart of the matter. And the heart of this book is the groping of a man, Leonard Cheshire, by trial and often error, to an understanding of the way to deal with the problem, a way which will make society better than it is, and perhaps make chronic sickness less terrible, both to its victims and to the healthy lookers-on.

CHAPTER TWO

LE COURT

IT WAS THE BEGINNING of 1948. Leonard Cheshire was twenty-nine. For some months he had been in the wilds of British Columbia, far from the whirl of plans and schemes for changing the world in which his dynamic energy had involved him since the end of the war. But, cutting short his badly needed holiday in Canada, came the summons to return to the dilapidated house in Hampshire which he had bought on mortgage not long before from an aunt. Here, barely a year ago, he had planted the battered remnants of his Christian Socialist experiment, "Vade in Pace" (known as V.I.P.). Within this movement, in the spring of 1946, he had gathered together a community of men and women, "in which," as he put it, "the strong would support the weak, the skilled the unskilled, the rich the poor, until all could stand on their own feet; in which, above all, the unity of purpose that had pulled us all through the war would prevail once more."

From the first the colony had run into many difficulties, not the least of them financial. At last, those who still remained had settled in this house in Hampshire, which was built on the slopes of a gentle hill overlooking some of the most beautiful country in England. Its name was the rather strange one of Le Court, pronounced in the English manner—Lea Court.

Cheshire had hoped—and so had his colonists—that they might get along for a year without him while he was in British Columbia. But it hadn't worked, so he had come back to them, and they decided, sadly, that the

V.I.P. experiment was no longer viable, and that they must give up. Cheshire took on himself the debts of the colony, and stayed on in the house with one faithful couple, wondering what to do next. Even his fertile, far-ranging imagination seemed to have dried up, for the first time since the beginning of his operational career as a twenty-year-old bomber pilot in the R.A.F. in 1940—that wartime career which has been described in other books, and which brought him the highest awards for bravery and culminated in the shattering experience of watching the second atom-bomb drop on Nagasaki.

He had tried many things in the hectic years since the end of the war; his health, despite the open-air months almost alone in a wild part of Canada, didn't seem to be too good; he felt he had let down the people who had put their faith and savings in his hands. He was thinking of religion—the religion his parents had given him, as established in the Church of England; and that didn't provide him with much comfort either. Now his Christian Socialist experiment had failed as well. It seemed that he was at the end of his tether—at twenty-nine.

One of the colonists, who had left Le Court when V.I.P. broke up, was an old man called Arthur Dykes. When news came one day about this time that Dykes was in hospital and wanted to see him, Cheshire could scarcely remember his face. Then he recalled the rather cantankerous old man who had looked after the pigs and had rubbed people up the wrong way; he was a withdrawn man who didn't talk much. Cheshire went over to the hospital and found Arthur making plans to get out of it. He wanted Cheshire to give him a small plot of land on the Le Court estate to build a bungalow, a pre-fab. Before they met in the ward, the Matron had asked Cheshire to see her first, and had told him that Arthur was dying of cancer. They couldn't keep him, for they could do nothing for him. Would the Group Captain find somewhere for him to go?

Cheshire thought it over, and then decided that he would, in fact must, find somewhere for the old man. But what should he tell him? "Can I tell him he is dying?" he asked the Matron. The answer was: "No."

So Cheshire chatted with Arthur, then left him, and spent a frantic week searching the county for a bed somewhere, anywhere. But it was no use, not even in a nursing-home at ten guineas a week, although where the ten guineas would have come from he didn't pause to think. And during their talk by Arthur's bedside the old man, with no home and no friends, had unwittingly revealed to Cheshire that for him Le Court was home—the only home he had ever known. Suddenly the solution dawned on Cheshire. Arthur must come to live out the last weeks of his life at Le Court.

Once he had made this decision, it followed logically that Arthur would have to be told the truth, whatever should be laid down to the contrary. Cheshire is a logical thinker, and a courageous one. Throughout this story there will be examples of what conventional minds will regard at best as irresponsibility, at worst as disobedience and disregard for good order and discipline. For my part I have always thought him to be a most disciplined man, who understands better than most the importance of obedience, provided there is logic behind the rules and regulations. He could see none in the case of Arthur Dykes.

"Arthur, I'm afraid they don't think there is anything they can do for you—in other words, they don't think you are going to get better."

Instead of being upset by the news, the old man welcomed it.

"Thanks, Len. It's a relief to know where I stand."

It had been the first time Arthur had called Cheshire by his Christian name. The ice was broken. He was then told there was no bed for him anywhere. Would he take a chance and come to Le Court? Somehow they would get along together. Cheshire, who had never nursed anyone in his life, took a few rudimentary lessons in changing sheets and giving a bed-bath. Then Arthur arrived. It can be said that the Cheshire Homes started from this moment in the spring of 1948. Cheshire himself had less idea than Arthur, oddly enough, that anything startling had happened. His experiments, after all, had been legion ever since he had left school, but they had all failed. Perhaps it was because this one started from outside himself rather than from inside that it would be different from all the others.

In the last week of June he had asked Arthur a point-blank question:

"What do you think of turning Le Court into a home for people like you—I mean, people who haven't anywhere to go and can't look after themselves?"

"Yes, Len. I think we ought to do it. I think God wants us to. And I think I could help you too."

Cheshire had not been able to conceal his astonishment that the old man, who was dying, should think he was able to help him. Then in a flash he saw how true this probably was. He couldn't help asking if Arthur had been thinking about it before, or whether it had been a sudden inspiration.

"Neither, really," had been the reply, "or I suppose I should say a bit of both. I hadn't actually thought of that idea, but I did feel that God couldn't have sent you along at that particular moment just for my good, and I was sort of waiting for something to happen. I rather felt you were too; you looked kind of lost."

The next thing in this important conversation, which contains much of the truth of the Cheshire movement, and some of the reasons for its later success, was a question by Arthur about how they should set about finding other homeless or sick people. Should they advertise?

Cheshire admitted that he hadn't thought ahead as

far as that. "I don't think we ought to take any action at all—just leave it in the hands of Providence and see what happens. If anyone turns up, we take them. If nobody turns up, we write off the idea."

He went on: "If patients turn up, we shan't have to worry about not having any money, shall we? We turn round to Providence and say: 'We haven't asked for them, so may we please have some money?' "

The end of this conversation came with a prophetic warning by the old man to the young one. It took the form of a question.

"But are you going to take anyone who turns up, no matter who they are—I mean, if they are all right, of course? Because you can't have it both ways, you know. You can't take the money God sends, unless you also take the patients He sends. I mean, if you're not going to run round refusing a cheque because it's too large—which you're not, are you?—can you refuse a patient just because he's too difficult or you're too busy? And that goes for the helpers too—for everything, in fact. If you're going to leave it to God, you'll have to play fair. Is that what you plan?"

"Oh yes, I'm quite prepared for all that. After all, it goes without saying, doesn't it?"

Arthur had looked pleased and quite satisfied, and today, fifteen years later, it is possible to say that Cheshire has kept faith with him, especially on this point—even to the extent, eventually, of setting up a new international organization under his own direct and personal control and that of his wife, when the success of his first concept had taken it, in some cases, in directions which he could neither approve of nor control; when the difficulties of nursing heavy cases, the expediency of putting money before the needs of the suffering, had distorted his idea until it was scarcely recognizable. Arthur Dykes seems to me to be a shining example of Providence working in extraordinary and unexpected ways. For this old man, who had never had a home of his own until the last months of his life, became the instrument for providing homes for so many people, both disabled and well, all over the world.

Then followed an extraordinary period in the few remaining weeks of Arthur Dykes's life. Cheshire tried to keep the rambling, empty house clean. There was scarcely any money to supplement Arthur's old age pension of twenty-five shillings a week. Cheshire's four hundred pounds a year pension as a retired Group Captain had been mortgaged for the rest of his life, so far as he could see, to meet the debts of V.I.P. Fortunately, there were fruit and vegetables in the garden, and, as usual, something always turned up at the last moment.

The second patient—in what had now become the first of the Homes—was Granny Haynes. She came as a result of a phone call from the porter at a block of flats in Knightsbridge, where another of Cheshire's aunts lived. Wilkins' grandmother-in-law had been bedridden for eighteen months. Her husband had suddenly been taken off to hospital, and Granny Haynes, in her fourth floor flat in Hammersmith, had nobody to look after her. She was ninety-one. Hesitantly, the porter asked Cheshire if he could possibly take her in. He could scarcely believe his ears when he heard that she could certainly come, and without filling up a form either. She had better bring some sheets, that was all. She came the next day.

One morning a local landowner dropped in at Le Court. He had heard of these strange beginnings. He was Honorary Treasurer of the Church Army. Cheshire told him of the idea that was dawning in his mind. He asked the friendly visitor whether he thought the Red Cross would be able to let him have some beds so that he could take in more people.

"Not the Red Cross. They don't touch beds—only

medical equipment. Try the Church Army. Mention my name."

The result of this was three lorry loads of furniture, including beds.

Arthur died on the 20th of August, 1948. Cheshire has left a vivid and moving account of his death in his book *The Face of Victory*. It was during the long vigil by the old man's death-bed that night, after he had carried out the last offices with difficulty, that he lighted on a book, *One Lord One Faith*, left on his desk by a casual visitor. The old man had been a Roman Catholic. This death-bed was undoubtedly one of the critical stages in Cheshire's life, and the book, by Monsignor Vernon Johnson, influenced him deeply. "For the first time in my experience," he writes, "someone was talking of truth and authority as the essence of religion." So Arthur Dykes died, and something came alive in Leonard Cheshire. It was not long before he was under instruction. Then he was received into the Roman Catholic Church.

A few days after Arthur's death, Ted was admitted. He had his left arm in plaster, and set in such a way that it was permanently erect, pointing up in the air above his head. You would have said he would be the last one to contribute to the running of Le Court, even if he had wished to do so. Cheshire says he was an outstanding example of how a severely disabled man could in fact more than pull his weight.

"Ted worked harder than any of us. He was immensely strong. He could heave a hundredweight sack of coal over his shoulder with his good arm. He used to look after the stove, and he did all the cutting of the grass in the garden—at least, he did the banks and I cut the lawn with a scythe. He was a marvellous chap."

Gradually the large house filled up with a strange variety of people—the disabled, the old, some T.B. cases, who were put in a separate part of the building, but were not segregated in any other way. There was no staff, apart from the owner and a growing number of visitors and voluntary helpers from the neighbourhood. The food was mostly from the garden, fresh but rather monotonous. The inevitable crisis came when two urgent applications arrived on the same day: a fifteen-stone man with paralysis about to be sent home from a hospital to his wife in a fourth-storey flat, and an ex-Marine in the British Legion in the final stages of meningitis. Here was the first test of the Cheshire Homes, the test which Arthur Dykes had foreseen—whether *anyone* in need was to be taken in—and appropriately the dilemma was put to the first patients; for there was no committee of management, no staff. It is a test which has not always been passed by admission and management committees in the years that followed. On this occasion, one strong character among the patients turned the tide, which had been running against acceptance.

In the event, neither man reached Le Court; they both died before they could arrive. And then Frances Jeram, almoner of a hospital in Portsmouth, who had somehow heard about the Group Captain, came to see for herself just what was going on at Le Court. She had discovered, in the course of her work, that it was almost impossible to find beds for T.B. convalescent cases, and that for people suffering from chronic illness there was just nowhere. Le Court wasn't far from Portsmouth, so she decided one evening after work to drive over there.

"I took my little car up that drive through the fields to the house. It was rather odd ringing the front-door bell. I had to wait for quite a long time. Then he opened the door and I had the surprise of my life. He seemed so different from what I had expected. He was so slight."

Cheshire took her into what they used to call the Peacock Room, and that evening she saw for the first time the strange gathering of young and old, chronic sick and T.B. cases, all eating their supper together, some with great difficulty, and Cheshire doling out the soup from a tureen at the head of the table.

She went back to Portsmouth, and the next day sent him one of her patients for whom she had been searching for a convalescent bed. Later there were one or two more; and as she wanted to make sure her own patients were happy in these experimental surroundings she used to drive over to Le Court after her work and stay on after supper talking with Cheshire, who found that her professional knowledge was something of which he was then very much in need.

"We used to sit up quite late by candlelight when the patients were all in bed. I remember him saying one evening that he saw a vista of many lights stretching away into the distance which would be Homes for the Sick all over England and the world."

Frances Jeram was able, during these talks, to show him that he could obtain grants for at least some of his patients from the County Health authorities under the new Health Act. She proposed to do so for those of her own patients whom she sent to him, and surely this would help? He was delighted, because the only money that was coming in was from the old age pensions of the handful who were drawing them. When he asked her if she would think of joining him and taking over the administration, she agreed at once. Next day she gave in her notice at her own hospital.

"I don't know whether you can understand it—a lot of people haven't been able to. I was terribly attracted, not to him so much, although the magic was certainly there, but to what he was trying to do."

At that time Cheshire's plans were changing all the time under the impact of new ideas and new impressions which flowed into his mind from the innumerable people with whom he was in contact. The job which Frances Jeram had been allotted changed at least once during the month of her notice with the Portsmouth Hospital;

in fact, she wasn't at all sure that it was still there, but then the situation came round full circle and she arrived in her van, having taken the precaution of bringing her own bed with her. It was as well. Cheshire had flown off to Switzerland. He had left word with Sister Anne, the T.B. case who was the only trained staff, about the room Mrs. Jeram was to occupy. When she was shown into it by the Sister, it was completely empty.

"The G.C. mentioned you would be coming and would be in charge. What shall we have for supper?"

"Let's see what's in the larder."

They went to the larder. The shelves were bare, apart from tea and sugar and two tins of spaghetti. And there were twelve people or more to feed. Next morning she went down to the grocer in the village. She found that Le Court already owed him nearly a hundred pounds.

For the next two and a half years Frances Jeram put her great devotion and courage into Le Court, and received no money for it. She will be remembered for two things particularly. It was her knowledge and training which laid the foundations of the partnership between the Ministry of Health, the County Health authorities and Cheshire in the matter of grants for patients in his Homes. It is on these grants that the movement has rested and grown in the United Kingdom. Secondly, an article which she was later to write for the *Almoner* was the spark which brought the new Le Court to life.

The arrival of Frances Jeram coincided with the first of the many spectacular incidents and symbolic gestures with which Cheshire has sprinkled the history of this movement.

Rosalind, an advanced case of T.B., had written to him from Singapore asking to be admitted to Le Court. He had accepted her. She had got as far as Zürich by rail and sea, only to be told by the airline which had booked her on to London that they could not take her further because of her illness. The other lines also refused to carry her to London. Desperately she telephoned Cheshire, for the airline had refused to refund her ticket money, and she had no more cash. Cheshire had none either, but he flew at once to Zürich, and overcame many obstacles erected by Continental bureaucracy. The hotel-keeper in Zürich realized that here was an exceptional situation, and used his own considerable influence. Cheshire brought Rosalind to Le Court in triumph by rail and boat. There was even an ambulance waiting for them at Victoria.

By the spring of 1949 there were twenty-nine patients at Le Court. Two significant things happened at this juncture. The story had by now gone round the circle of professional almoners, especially in the London hospitals, that a young ex-R.A.F. pilot was taking disabled and chronic sick people into his own house and nursing them himself. No rules, no red tape, no money, apparently. Cherry Morris, the almoner with whom this story began, had always worked for the chronic sick, especially the young sufferers. She had realized for some time that little, if anything, was being done for them because little enough was known about them. Was this curious story true?

She went down to Le Court, and her description of what she found goes right to the heart of the matter.

"The house seemed to be in a pretty poor state of repair. There were about thirty patients of all kinds. It made no sense at all from the conventional point of view, but the spirit was quite amazing. There was no pause between the staff and the patients."

I think professional people must find it difficult, if not impossible, to see this kind of situation in focus. All their training and experience cries out against it. But this woman was at the top of her profession, and she understood in a flash. There was no pause between the wheeler and the wheeled.

Before this happened Le Court was visited by the Press. A reporter from the *News Chronicle* came down. Cheshire had opposed Press publicity. His principal reason was that he wanted to be quite sure that he was acting within the limits laid down by Providence, and was not merely following a whim of his own. But on the 10th of September there was an article on the front page. It was a Saturday. On the Monday morning the post was heavy. Cheshire had to call for help in dealing with it. A friend who had kept the accounts of V.I.P. was living at Liss and coming over from time to time. He started opening the pile. The first letter contained two pound notes. He was astounded, and said so.

"I've had two or three like that too," was Cheshire's response.

They were still counting the cash at ten o'clock that night—seven hundred and twenty pounds.

The next day, Tuesday, the front-door bell rang. It was a blind man and a woman. They asked if they could come in and speak to Group Captain Cheshire. They explained that they had read the article in the *News Chronicle*. They had felt certain he would receive many letters which would need answering. They had a typewriter with them, which the man could use. Could they help with the acknowledgements?

"There were far more letters to write than I could cope with. We had no typewriter, and even if we had owned one nobody could have used it. So we got down to it right away. I composed four or five standard thank-you's, and added a personal paragraph at the end of each letter. The woman read them out and the man typed them. We got through them all in the day. Then they went away. I never knew their names."

Then, as so often in the years to come, just when the ship seemed to be settling down on an even keel, Cheshire left his little band to fend for themselves. They were forlorn and not a little upset. This time it was his health, which seemed about to break down and demanded that he should have a change. Sir Charles Symons, who had advised him to give up the R.A.F. as a career after the war, saw him again now, and told him he would have to take up a regular job. Le Court was getting the better of him. He must leave it for a time to others.

This was the first, and probably the most exacting, crisis that Cheshire had to face, for it was a personal one. What was he going to do about Le Court now that he had been ordered to leave it? His first thoughts were concerned with the doctor's orders. Did he have to obey them? But the last months had got him down more than anything in his life hitherto.

"When you are down, somehow the tendency seems to be to get even further submerged. That's how I was at this time. To disobey the doctors would have been flying against Providence. I decided to give in."

This was how he described it many years later. But he couldn't just go away and leave them—the patients, Frances Jeram, and all the people who had been in it with him. They all talked it over, round and round. The conclusion was inescapable. Le Court must be run by a committee.

"It was the hardest thing for me. I hated the idea of a committee. It was like what I imagine a mother must feel if she has to hand her child over to others, even if they are friends; and even at the last minute I struggled against this decision, but there was no other way. That was my first lesson, the need to decentralise, to hand over to others something I had started myself. It doesn't sound much now, but it was terribly hard at the time."

The next crisis came almost at once. The committee accepted the responsibility for looking after the Home in his absence, but they attached a condition to this acceptance—that it should be known as the Cheshire Home at Le Court. His name must be linked with it, for they felt certain that without it they would not be able to raise funds to keep it going. Cheshire was horrified at the idea. He remonstrated and pleaded with them, but they were adamant.

Looking back, it is easy to see both points of view. In the years that have gone by since then, it has been possible to point to occasions when the temptation to use his name and its associations has been too great for some of his supporters, so that the spirit of his work has been overlaid by the too easy, catchpenny use of his name. On the other hand, who can deny that inspiration by itself, no matter how great the flow of voluntary help, is not enough to turn stately houses into nursing homes, or to conjure new buildings out of thin air? With a sigh he bowed to the inevitable. It would be the Cheshire Home at Le Court.

Shortly before he went away his father and mother came to live in Laundry Cottage on the Le Court estate. His war achievements had always given his mother justifiable pride as well as immense and understandable anxiety, and she now took a growing interest in what he was trying to do. Gradually, with his father, she came to occupy a unique place in his organization, which brought her great happiness as well as comfort and encouragement to his growing family of patients.

His father soon came to the conclusion that he had better keep this latest venture of his son from going the way of so many of its predecessors. He had been Professor of Law at Oxford, and he persuaded one of his former pupils, Sir Alfred Denning, as he then was, to become chairman of a managing committee. In the intervening years, many distinguished lawyers from this country and overseas have become connected with Professor Cheshire's son and his work for the sick.

The small body which had already been formed to look after the day-to-day affairs of Le Court was quite distinct from this new managing body, which would be a Trust, with its own Articles of Association, called The Cheshire Foundation Homes for the Sick. It came into existence so that there should be a legal entity to which the Home could be conveyed, and which would be responsible to the public for the wise use of its donations. The idea of a Trust had been in the air since the beginning of this year, 1952. Its first meeting took place at Laundry Cottage on Sunday, 30th March. Of the five original members, only three could get there because of the snow—Professor Cheshire, Sir Alfred Denning and Cheshire himself.

Here began the process of giving the work due form and order, and of enshrining its spirit in a definable and lasting constitution. Here began the conflict which could never be truly resolved at any time in the future between Cheshire's unpredictable, soaring spirit and the businesslike, pedestrian caution of his followers. He was to be more tolerant of their caution than many of them would be of his adventures, for he recognized always that the human soul cannot operate in this world without a body, and that a body without a soul is a lifeless organism. So it would be for him from now on. The Cheshire Foundation and Cheshire himself would be necessary and complementary to each other. He knew, too, that inevitably they would be at war with each other. The story, as it unfolds, will show how unerring was his instinct at this time.

The decision has also a vital bearing on the religious element in the Homes. From the moment his father stepped into the affairs of Le Court and brought Sir Alfred Denning with him, it was clear that Cheshire himself had decided that his work for the sick, however it was to develop, must grow in an atmosphere of religious harmony. It had all begun at the time of his own decision to become a Roman Catholic, and its extraordinary success was for him part of the new life, the new happiness. So long as he had anything to do with it, God would be in his Homes, although he had no inclination to ram religion down anybody's throat. But because he had become a Roman Catholic there were not lacking people who jumped to the conclusion that the whole thing would now become an appendage of Rome. The answer should have been clear. He would not have left this child of his imagination and his luck in the hands of Anglicans, such as his father and Sir Alfred Denning, while he disappeared from the scene, if he had been thinking at any time in those early days of making it a denominational movement.

It was during the winter preceding the formation of the Trust that bad news had come about the subsidence of the foundations at Le Court. Men digging in the basement discovered that its foundations were being eaten away by an underground stream. At least six thousand pounds would have to be spent to make the house safe to live in.

About this time Frances Jeram, who was still in charge of the patients at Le Court, wrote the article for the *Almoner* which has already been referred to, in response to the numerous questions she was being asked. A young almoner read it and took it to her father, Sir George Dyson, who was head of the Royal Academy of Music and a Trustee of the United Kingdom Carnegie Trust. She urged her father to persuade the Carnegie Trust to do something for the exciting venture at Le Court. Sir George agreed to see Frances Jeram.

"I felt very diffident," she said later, "sitting in his big room at the Royal Academy, where the only piece of furniture was a large grand piano. He asked me what I thought we needed most. I said at once I thought some form of central heating, because we were never warm in winter. There was no money for coal, and it wasn't too often that Toc H could come to cut down trees for firewood. I said I thought the cost would be about four hundred pounds for doing some of the downstairs rooms.

" 'My dear,' Sir George had said, 'I'm afraid we were thinking in rather bigger terms than that.'

"I was very abashed, and didn't quite know what to say."

Then she told the story of Sir George's visit to Le Court with two of his fellow Trustees.

"It was rather awful, because I couldn't get Leonard to play. He didn't seem interested at first, and as it was all my fault I felt responsible. We hadn't really got enough spoons and forks except for one end of the table, and I remember getting some of our own stuff out of store. Then there was the lavatory, always a bit of a problem with us, as you can imagine. The best one downstairs had to be kept shut all the morning. And then when they came Leonard wouldn't give up what he was doing to come and talk to them before lunch. When he did come, of course, he was so charming he captivated them. There was no talk about anything to do with Le Court at lunch, but afterwards they went out into the garden and Sir George asked him where he would site a new house—just like that. Leonard said quickly enough, 'Over there', pointing to the eastern side of the house, so I suppose he had been thinking of the possibility. Then I faded out of the picture."

Cheshire was asked to go to Berwick to meet the other members of the Carnegie Trust. From the moment he was in personal contact with them across a table it was practically all over. The Trustees agreed to make available sixty-five thousand pounds for a new building on the Le Court estate which would be designed specifically for the chronic sick and the badly disabled, with the advice of the pioneer patients. The building finally cost seventy-five thousand pounds. Cheshire was astonished at the goodwill of the Trustees of the Carnegie Foundation. Both they and he had been given to suppose that the new Le Court would cost considerably less, but although the final cost came as a surprise to the Trustees they nevertheless decided to go ahead with the scheme. To Cheshire the additional cost came as a shock, since it represented such a great departure from the way in which he had worked up to that moment.

When he left Le Court he went to a job which came to him through his old friend and chief of Bomber Command days, Sir Ralph Cochrane. It was to be with Vickers Armstrong, on the aviation side. Although some people imagined it was a flying job, in fact he was to be an administrator on the ground. The work took him, to begin with, to Weybridge to work with Barnes Wallis, the inventor, who had designed the dam-busting bombs which had been lobbed from a hundred and fifty feet, with devastating effect, at the Moehne and Eder dams in the Ruhr by Guy Gibson and the crews of 617 Squadron. Cheshire had taken over command of this Squadron after Gibson's death. He had also dropped a number of tallboys on Germany himself—the ten-ton block-busters designed by the man he was now to work for. His new job took him from Weybridge to Culdrose airfield, near Penzance. There he was able to scrounge an old Spitfire, which he took up as often as his work allowed. It helped him to blow away the cobwebs; it also enabled him to fly back to Weybridge at week-ends, so that he could visit Le Court and preside over the meetings of his committee. He would beat up Le Court regularly on Saturdays to let everyone know he was coming home. And then his week-end visits became noticeably fewer, until they almost ceased. Soon the news was out. Everyone at Le Court knew about it. He was starting a new Home on the Lizard.

Poking round a deserted Coastal Command airfield at Predannack, on the Lizard peninsula, he had found an empty hut made of concrete blocks with an asbestos cement roof. Cows had wandered in there often during the Cornish winters since the Coastal Command squadrons had faded away in 1945. It was dark and deserted, and grass was growing up through the cracks in the floor. With his flair for firing people to do things they would never have dreamed of doing on their own, he persuaded one or two people to help him clear up the hut, and so make it habitable.

At first he seems to have been working round it almost on his own. An odd-job man was watching him trying to lay bricks. He was doing it so badly that the man could stand it no longer and showed him how it should be done. From then on he became part of the organization. Others who had come to look stayed to work—glazing windows, painting walls and repairing the broken-down furniture. Culdrose aerodrome played its part. A bulldozer turned up to clear the ground for a sewage tank which was lowered into position by a crane, which also came by at the right moment. As sometimes happens, a gift didn't work and became an embarrassment—in this case an ancient Aga cooker someone had dumped on him. The man who came to give an estimate for putting it right took one look and pronounced it fit only for the scrap-heap. Before he went on his way Cheshire showed him round. The rooms had been freshly painted by volunteers, there were curtains at the windows. It was beginning to take shape. As he started up his van the man said:

"On second thoughts, we'll have a shot at that cooker. It might work."

In May, 1952, the first three patients and three staff arrived. Cheshire called the hut St. Teresa's. The sight of three disabled Cornish people actually in the transformed hut, warm and comfortable, was an inspiration not only to the people of the Lizard, but to many others in the county. Unlike the early days at Le Court, Cheshire had no local prejudices to overcome because of the failure of an earlier enterprise: V.I.P. and its trail of debts had made the start at Le Court that much harder. In Cornwall he began from scratch; and although a dispersal hut might have seemed, to those onlookers who so soon became involved themselves, the most unpromising material out of which to make a Home for the sick, Cheshire had acquired considerable expertise in his "do it yourself" technique. Allied to his undiminished skill in persuading others to work for him, this technique succeeded more rapidly in Cornwall than in Hampshire. At just about the time when Vickers made him an extremely generous offer to continue working for them, he decided to give up the job altogether. He was not at all clear in his mind how he should go about his own personal work. He only knew that the care of the sick was now what he had to do.

Lady St. Levan, whose husband is a local landowner and who is influential in the county, was one of the first visitors. She was taken aback by what she saw; but she realized that, despite its shaky foundations and almost non-existent finances, both of which might justify the authorities in closing it down, there was nevertheless a spark which must be kept alive. She got in touch with Alderman Stephens, the Mayor of Penzance, and persuaded him to visit the hut at Predannack. A convoy of fifteen cars left the Mayor's parlour to visit the hut on the Lizard. He and his wife were so shocked at the sight of the patients—they had never realized that such people existed—that when they returned home they were unable to eat their supper. They vowed that they would not rest until they had built a new and proper home for them in better surroundings.

Their first decision was that land must be found nearer Penzance, and funds must be collected to build an entirely new building. So every evening Alderman Stephens drove round the countryside he knew so well looking for a site. One night he turned off the main road from Penzance along the shore of Mount's Bay up a side road which connects it with the A.30 from Penzance to Hayle. On the skyline to the right was a copse of pine trees, which at that point masked his view of St. Michael's Mount, the lovely castle on its little island dominating the wide sweep of the bay. It was the home of Lady St. Levan. Between the road and the pines was a fairly extensive piece of what appeared to be waste land covered with gorse bushes. He got out of the car, climbed over a stile and walked round it. Surely this was the spot? Whom did it belong to? In fact, he had a pretty good idea that it belonged to the owner of St. Michael's Mount. He drove home and telephoned Lady St. Levan. Her husband's family had lived at the Mount for over three centuries. She would probably know something about this land. So he described it on the telephone.

"I'll ask my husband. He's almost sure to know who it belongs to."

He did. It belonged to him. And not only did he make it over to the committee by a deed of gift, but when the new single-storey, specially designed Home had been built with funds raised from the people of Cornwall, he cut a gap through the copse of pine trees so that the patients could see the Mount, with its outline of turrets and the roof of the chapel, across the intervening distance of land and sea, framed in the trees which now belonged to them.

Then once again events took charge. Cheshire collapsed at his new Home, and was taken to the hospital at Hayle. The diagnosis was clear. He had tuberculosis. He was taken from Hayle in Cornwall to the sanatorium at Midhurst in Surrey, where he was to stay for the next two years.

CHAPTER THREE

SAINT CECILIA'S

CHESHIRE WAS IN the Midhurst sanatorium from August, 1952, until the winter of 1954. During this time he had four severe operations, and for part of it he was very ill. He had no intention, despite his predicament, of leading the passive life of a very sick person. Placed in much the same situation as many of those whom he had been trying to help at Le Court and the Lizard, he did instinctively what he had been trying to get his disabled friends to do—lead a full life of the mind and spirit. It says much for Sir Geoffrey Todd and the staff at Midhurst that they acquiesced in this departure from normal practice.

Rest, quiet, no visitors, no excitement seem to have been the traditional routine for T.B. patients at that period, and I suppose it still is for the happily dwindling numbers of people suffering from this disease. Cheshire demonstrated that the opposite suited him, except, of course, that he was stuck in bed for a long time.

This scarcely mattered to a man who had been involved through the war years with scientific gadgets. Today we are familiar with tape-recorders and office equipment of every sort and kind, but as recently as 1952 they were unheard of in England outside the pile-carpeted corridors of the captains of industry. Cheshire had been using them for some time to cut down his dependence on the physical presence of secretaries and stenographers. Besides, they helped him to economize, for tapes could be handed over to voluntary workers to type in their spare time.

His room at Midhurst was like a modern office, with dictating machines and piles of tapes and correspondence—people were now writing to him from all over the country, some of them disabled men and women asking for a bed in one of his Homes. Then there were the two Homes.

He was confident, at the moment when it seemed he could do nothing further about it, that he had stumbled on a gap in the elaborate structure of the Health Service. But was this illness to be the sudden ending of his latest experiment, which had been more successful than any of the others, but was yet perhaps doomed to failure by his own disability? Or was it a sign that he should give up active work in this new field? Should he leave it to more practical people to carry on where he had shown the way?

His time in Midhurst, despite the bustle of the sick-room, was a period of reflection, an involuntary and prolonged retreat. What the months of solitude and wood-cutting in British Columbia had failed to do the enforced incarceration in the sanatorium succeeded in achieving; but there were doubts in his mind. Before his illness he had visited the monastery at Solesmes in France, and had felt attracted to the idea of becoming a monk so that he could pass his life in prayer for his Homes, leaving them to grow under the impetus of more practical people than himself. But even before he could consider this possibility as anything but a distant dream, he had to get better. He had no means then of knowing whether he might not be in a sanatorium for ten years, maybe for life.

One of the most striking things for me about Cheshire is his relaxed pursuit of his objectives. This does not mean that the pursuit is not relentless, for it is; but he never seems to strain after the immediate end. His almost poker-playing technique gives the impression that he couldn't care less whether he gets what he wants or not.

Frances Jeram had painted that vivid picture of his apparent indifference to a successful outcome for Le Court when she described the visit of Sir George Dyson and the Trustees of the Carnegie Foundation.

One explanation of this apparent indifference to the successful outcome of the immediate issue in hand may lie in his unwillingness to consider the attainment of his objectives except on his own terms. Since conditions are attached to most things and his lack of attachment is so genuine, this apparent indifference to success has sometimes resulted in the very conditions to which he objected being waived. Only occasionally, as we shall see, and on the biggest issues, did he have to compromise.

This characteristic was apparent now at Midhurst in relation to the growth of the Homes. He must have hoped inwardly that the whole business had not come to a full stop, but he certainly did nothing overt to encourage the birth of new ventures.

It was during this mood of reflection and withdrawal that the Bromley Home started.

One day in 1953 he received a letter from a boy at Chislehurst in Kent. Richard was eight. The other boys in his class at school were collecting autographs of the famous fighter and bomber pilots of the war. He had decided to write to Group Captain Cheshire. Sadly, the letter arrived at a moment when he was particularly ill, and it lay unanswered with the many others that were flowing in from all over the country and from abroad. But as soon as he could tackle his correspondence again, Cheshire answered this letter. He explained how sorry he was for the delay, but he was ill in hospital and sometimes got a bit behindhand with his letters. That was all.

The little boy decided to continue the correspondence. He wrote back to Midhurst saying they had a very good crop of raspberries in the garden of their house at Chislehurst, and would Group Captain Cheshire like some? The answer came by return. "Yes, please." So at the week-end his parents drove with their son to Midhurst and left a large basket of raspberries with the receptionist. They were just driving off when a nurse came down and said the patient would like to see them. Richard would have to stay outside the window.

The father, Bob Worthington, told me later of this meeting. "His room was more like an office; there were dictating machines, tapes, letters and books all over the place; the atmosphere was full of bustle and activity. I remember we talked a little about recording machines and their characteristics, and I told him I worked for a firm which manufactured one type of recording tape. He took me up on this soon afterwards, because he was interested in recording church music. We sent some technicians down to Midhurst to see him."

At that first meeting nothing much happened. Richard carried on a brief conversation with Cheshire through the window about the raspberries. His father did feel, I think, the atmosphere of inner calm which prevailed through the bustle of the room. He remembered the large photograph on the wall opposite the bed of a very beautiful face, which he later learned was a reproduction of the face on the Holy Shroud at Turin, reputedly the winding sheet of our Lord left empty at the tomb of Gethsemane.

The idea of a Home in Bromley grew from the visits of this couple to Midhurst. During these talks Cheshire emphasized the importance which he attached to saving every penny on buildings, on alterations, if they should be necessary, and in planning. It is easy to see how this emphasis on economy must have permeated all his thinking, as he looked back on the early days of poverty and of struggling against odds at Le Court; in fact, Le Court was still not out of the wood, although the committee was growing in confidence and had already held the first garden fête, at which they had cleared over three hundred pounds.

"It will have to be an old house. New houses are expensive and we haven't got any money," he had said to Bob's wife, when she told him she would start looking for a suitable house in the Bromley area.

Another thing he had urged them to do was to accept patients just as soon as it should be possible. He had seen how this moulding process had taken place at Le Court and in even more rugged surroundings in the hut on the windy perimeter of Predannack airfield. It could be done and he knew it was the right way, whatever the cult of the Welfare State might indicate to the contrary. The new Le Court, with its specially designed lift, the wide corridors with the handrails along the walls, the bathrooms with the special aids, these would be all right because the Home had started without them; the patients would bring their real home with them from the old house, the home they had built up from shared memories of difficulties surmounted by faith, team work and leadership. Nevertheless, years later he told me how much the patients hated it when the time came to leave the old building. As if to underline the truth of this, the house put up an obstinate fight against the pick-axes of the demolishers.

One fact of which he became aware during this time of reflection was that most people at every level of society in Britain had as much of the spirit of voluntary service as ever, and this despite the widespread belief, in the immediate post-war years, that planning by the men in Whitehall and in the town hall was better for everybody than individual effort and decision. In the wider field of government and reconstruction after the war this may have been true—certainly the British people had opted for a planned society by an overwhelming vote. But in some of the traditional fields of free enterprise it didn't look at this time, any more than it does now, as if bureaucracy was the right answer.

In the matter of the severely disabled, it seemed to

Cheshire that the new giant of the Health Service would not have the time or the perception to handle the problem properly. In fact, the giant hadn't even noticed it. Cheshire sensed that there were thousands, perhaps tens of thousands, who could still believe in the Welfare State, yet give wholeheartedly of their spare time and skills to the problem on which he had stumbled by accident.

So the mother of the boy who had written for his autograph set about looking for an old, and at the same time a cheap, house in the Chislehurst/Bromley area on the south-eastern outskirts of London. Before she had found anything, Cheshire from his sick-bed asked her husband if he would help with a scheme which might appear to be divorced from the chronic sick and the Homes, but which in fact was its counterpart in the realm of spiritual healing.

A fellow patient and an ex-Bomber Command pilot had offered him two old Bedford buses for which he had no further use. Cheshire had accepted them gladly. He now planned to use one of the buses to put over to the public at large an influence of a spiritual kind parallel to the work the Homes were doing on the physical plane. He had the interior of one of them ripped out so that there was room for a series of tableaux—Advent, the Nativity, Lent, Easter and finally the Holy Shroud of Turin. There were at different times some doves, a lamb—which Bob Worthington kept in his garden—a loudspeaker unit which relayed church music, and messages about the New Testament and about Cheshire's religious belief, which was now built on the rock of his newly found faith.

The process of thought in his mind ran on these lines: whatever we do in life must be related to our final end, so that, if we are to give everything we do its true meaning, we must know what the purpose of life is. Good works, however excellent, are not enough: to provide the sick and homeless with houses and attention is a waste of time, unless in the doing of it both those who help and those who are helped come closer to the attainment of their life's goal. We have been endowed with minds with which to pursue and attain truth, and with a will with which to work out and adhere to what is good; and since we are capable of loving what we think is good but in fact is not, the one thing that really matters is the pursuit of truth, to which nothing may be subordinated, not even the relief of suffering.

The old Bedford, which finished its remarkable life six years later at the hands of car thieves, has handed over its task of making known the Holy Shroud of Turin—and through it something of the inner meaning of suffering—to other and more modern media. Its work still goes on with increasing success, never meeting any acrimony or irreverence, in spite of its religious nature—in itself an astonishing testimony to the value of the message which the Shroud has to tell. In this way the Cheshire movement, even at this early and controversial stage, was working towards the unity in which its founder believed, that unity which can only be based on a common acceptance of truth, as God has revealed it.

From his bedside Cheshire recruited a small, mixed Anglican-Roman Catholic crew of friends to man the bus, notably one of his strongest supporters down in Cornwall, a girl in the Women's Auxiliary Corps called Shelagh Howe. Bob, who is an Anglican, agreed to be skipper. On many mornings of that winter of 1953-4 it was driven up to London and parked in a side street behind Oxford Street, to be picked up after work by the crew. It would then be driven in the rush hour to the most crowded spot in the most crowded street, and Cheshire's voice from his bed in Midhurst would float over the loudspeaker to the hurrying crowds, some of whom stopped to listen.

In the middle of the winter Cheshire sent them a

full-length photograph of the Holy Shroud with its remarkable imprint of a face and body bearing the marks of apparent crucifixion. Bob thought the atmosphere of the bus and its contents were beginning to reflect the rituals of the Roman Catholic Church. It would have been rather surprising if they had not, in view of the deep happiness Cheshire continued to derive from his religion. But I am sure it was as true then as I know it to be today that he did not plan deliberate conversion of those around him to the religion he had himself embraced.

I talked with Cheshire later about this, as we had to do, for this period of the story was a controversial one.

"Naturally, I believe in the one true Church. I wouldn't have asked to be received into it if I hadn't. Naturally I should be happy if you were to join it, because I believe it to be the one true Church founded by our Lord; but I shouldn't try to force you into it, if I thought you didn't want to come."

It was now May, 1954. Bob's wife had found a house in Sundridge Avenue, Bromley, which she and her husband thought might be a possible starter for a Home, although the price, at eight thousand pounds, was high. It had a garden and a number of rooms on three floors. As they had no experience of what was wanted, they suggested that Cheshire might spend a week-end with them to see the house, if he were allowed out of the sanatorium.

It was his first exeat since his admission to Midhurst eighteen months before. He had an open wound in his chest with a tube in it. He had to rest at regular intervals on his back, and the wound had to be dressed twice a day.

He came on Saturday morning. After a rest and the first dressing they all went to see the house. He looked it over with an experienced eye and found it not very suitable—too many narrow passages, no natural place for a lift, and difficult stairs. But he thought it would just about do, if the price could be brought down. He only had sixty pounds in the world, which they could have for a start. Then he seemed to forget about it.

That week-end, on the spur of the moment, and to some extent as a result of Bob's asking him if he had ever been there, three of them set out at two hours' notice, in a chartered aircraft, for Lourdes—Bob, a Protestant; Father Fuller, a Roman Catholic priest from London; and Cheshire. For twenty-four hours he went through the whole process of a normal pilgrimage, including immersion; and this with a tube in his chest. There was no rest and there were no dressings, yet he experienced an exaltation of the spirit which he had not felt before and which he determined to bring from then on to as many in England as he could, especially to those in the Homes, who found it difficult and expensive to make this pilgrimage. When he got back, with the help of Bob, Shelagh Howe and the others, Cheshire laid on regular air charters to Lourdes every summer and autumn for the sick and for those who wanted to go on behalf of someone else in need. They are still being flown nearly ten years after this, his first pilgrimage.

Lourdes seems to him to make a unique contribution by helping people to bear their sufferings. Put in another way, it helps them to place suffering in its right perspective. As he sees it, there are miracles at Lourdes from time to time, but these are infrequent and not the real point of Lourdes. The real miracle is something different.

A pilgrim will go there with expense and difficulty, desperately hoping for a cure. On arriving and seeing others worse off than himself, he begins to wish that they too will be cured. Before long he finds himself wishing that they will be cured before he is himself; and finally he comes away pleased that he wasn't himself cured, and determined not to hope for a cure any more. For Cheshire this is the greatest happiness and the true miracle.

Before returning to Midhurst on the Tuesday morning, he went to the bank in Bromley. The sellers agreed to bring the price of the house down to half their original asking bid, and a mortgage was arranged. Cheshire drew out most of the mortgage money, and the house was purchased. Already there was a small committee, which had met in the Worthingtons' home on the evening before the flight to Lourdes. Public opinion in the neighbourhood was being mobilized. Cheshire then handed over his own sixty pounds, which was the only cash the committee had to start with. Having done this, he returned to bed, and soon underwent the most severe operation of his whole time at the sanatorium.

The starting of St. Cecilia's,* the name given by Cheshire to the Bromley Home, is one of the most interesting of the story for two reasons. First, Cheshire's own presence and the leadership he was normally able to exert were almost wholly absent. In fact, the long week-end of the 24th May was the only time he appeared on the scene. Secondly, there seems little doubt that the divisions which became manifest among the first management committee, and which were largely due to clashes of personality, were attributed by some people to religious differences. This misconception might easily have wrecked the new venture.

During the autumn of 1954 the house in Bromley became the centre of much activity, nearly all of it voluntary. Cheshire's idea of "do it yourself" had caught on. Rotary Clubs, Round Tables, Youth Clubs, Boy Scouts and Girl Guides rallied to a cause they could understand, for while these enthusiastic young people were scrubbing floors, painting walls, working in the garden and humping furniture, they could see the end to which all this activity was directed; for there were already several patients waiting to enter the Home. It

* Cheshire called the Home after the patrician lady of Sicily who was executed by Marcus Aurelius because of her conversion to Christianity, for his decision finally to remain in the world and not to become a monk had been made on the 22nd November, St. Cecilia's Day. He had decided then that if there should be another Home he would like to name it after this courageous early Christian martyr.

was an organism that was coming to life under their very eyes and with their own help.

At first there were only three patients, and the money situation, as usual, was difficult. One or two prominent men in the City heard of the venture. One of them in particular, Sir Archibald Jamieson, sensed that there was something novel and exciting in the deliberate way this group of people living in a suburb of London had taken risks which were quite out of the ordinary. Sir Archibald was a merchant banker. He also knew about men, and one of his sons had been awarded a posthumous V.C. He decided to back the Cheshire idea, and subscribed a considerable sum. It was an important and generous decision. Much was to flow from it both for St. Cecilia's and for the Cheshire Homes in general.

Not long afterwards Cheshire asked Sir Alfred Denning if the Foundation would agree to take St. Cecilia's under its wing. The local committee was anxious that this should happen, and the Foundation agreed. Le Court had already sent them beds and linen, and many of the essentials needed for starting up. These gifts had been gratefully received both for their intrinsic usefulness and as a sign that the new committee could count on the friendship and support of the first Home. Cheshire's own sixty pounds hadn't gone very far.

It was natural that Sir Archibald, who had proved such a generous benefactor, and had such a profound experience of business, should join the Trustees of the Foundation. He was asked to become the Honorary Treasurer. As there was nothing to take over in the way of cash, he paid another capital sum into the account with the Westminster Bank, half of which was a gift from himself and half from a friend who wished to remain anonymous. They both asked that the money should be spent, when the time was ripe, on improvements to St. Cecilia's.

So the new Home had come into existence without

Cheshire's volition and without his personal inspiration. While it was growing up with its own committee of management, and while this committee of people whom he hardly knew had agreed to become part of a bigger organization presided over by more people he knew only a little better, he was forced to stay in his bed in the sanatorium.

He had already made the big decision to return to the world when the doctors would let him—for it was clear by now that his health would make this possible, although he would only have one lung. During the last half of his sojourn in the sanatorium he had to make another decision. This time he was helped by the advice he received from the Roman Catholic Bishops, and later from Cardinal Gracias.

He had thought during his last months in bed that it would be right to set up a second body, alongside the Cheshire Foundation Homes for the Sick, which would look after the more difficult and specialized patients not likely to be admitted by the Foundation. These, he felt, could best be looked after by a Catholic organization manned by people who felt dedicated to the task.

The point at issue in his mind was that already the new Trust, practical and efficient, was limiting the intake of patients to certain well-defined categories. The dying, T.B. cases and mental patients were being firmly excluded, and the old, too, were not very popular.

It was the beginning of this inevitable rift between himself and his more cautious supporters which had caused him in 1951, before he went to Midhurst, to start his third Home, Holy Cross, in a Cornish farmhouse near St. Teresa's. It was here that he had put an ex-Bomber pilot who had become schizophrenic, whose mother could no longer look after him, and for whom the R.A.F. Association could not find a place. Cheshire had first taken him into St. Teresa's as an emergency case, but it had soon become clear that he couldn't stay there with the other patients, so either he had to be sent away or Cheshire had to start a new Home for him. He did what he was always to do. But because of his limited means he could only take what was immediately to hand, a farmhouse a few miles away. Inevitably this led to trouble: for once St. Teresa's had settled down and been taken over by a committee the ex-goalbirds, social misfits and schizophrenics who found their home at nearby Holy Cross were not acceptable as neighbours of the more conventional St. Teresa's. When St. Teresa's was moved to the land near Penzance given by Lord St. Levan, and a new building put up with money donated by the people of Cornwall, Cheshire was forced to abandon Holy Cross, owing to lack of support. Shelagh Howe, his friend in the Women's Auxiliary Corps, gallantly took it on and has been running it ever since in her own name.

One can detect in this early experiment the beginnings of the international settlements which he and his wife were to found ten years later in India and other countries. He would never give up the idea on which his movement was based—in no circumstances to refuse a case, however hard the nursing might be. His compassion for the dying and the sorely stricken was never to be turned aside by expediency or difficulties. Here at the beginning of his work he was compelled to yield by his practical helpers, but his strategy remained firmly fixed in his mind, even if the tactics he had sought to use—a separate Roman Catholic Trust—proved, by his own admission, to be faulty.

Curiously enough, it was the Catholic Church herself who advised him against such a Trust. He had started off, he was told, on this new venture which had begun so well by appealing for support to people of all religions, and had thereby awoken a response which had surprised many. Although he had never asked for it, he had received considerable support both in voluntary help and in money; and it would be wrong to do anything which would give the appearance that the whole venture was not entirely undenominational. Later, when he went to India, Cardinal Gracias, the Indian Cardinal, gave him the same advice.

This, then, was the next decision of this Midhurst period—that, even though the Cheshire Homes did not embrace all that Cheshire intended to do, the entire work should remain non-denominational.

But he had yet to appreciate to the full the deep pain of parting with direct control of his creation and child. Handing over the old Le Court to its first committee had been painful indeed. Before he left Midhurst he had to agree to a condition which the Carnegie Trust insisted on as a basis for their grant, and without which the new Le Court could not be built. Cheshire would have to agree in writing that he would never wield any personal control over Le Court, and never undertake any work or build any building on the Le Court estate on his own initiative.

He has always hated being tied down by conditions or agreements which might fetter his freedom of action. He was all for rejecting the offer.

"I was sure we could get the money somewhere else without any conditions, and even if we couldn't our freedom and independence were more important than a new building."

He spent all one afternoon at Midhurst composing letters of refusal, but none of them seemed to come right. One by one he tore them all up. When the time came for handing over the letter to the sister for posting, he had made himself ill again. Then he knew he must give in. He wrote four lines accepting.

Five years later, in 1959, the B.B.C. made a full-length film of his work up to that time. When they reached this stage in the story, the camera travelled from the old house, which was half demolished, to the beautiful new building that had been erected a hundred yards to the east. The contrast between the two buildings represented, in bricks and mortar, the contrast between poverty and riches which was to characterize the Cheshire movement from now on.

I have always sensed that in Cheshire's view something was lost when the new Le Court replaced the old; more especially because of his shock at what he considered to be the excessive cost of the new building, and his feeling that somehow he had inadvertently taken advantage of the generosity of the Carnegie Trust.

But although something was perhaps lost, clearly there was an overall nett gain, for it was indeed true, as the B.B.C. commentator was to say, that "Le Court was to become the spearhead of an enterprise which would spread through the British Isles and the whole world". And the new Le Court would on at least one occasion provide the material necessities of the spearhead, as the old Le Court would always provide the spiritual inspiration.

This was a difficult period for Cheshire, when he was trying to work out the basis for the future of his numerous activities. Because he saw his work as under the direction of Providence, not of merely human planning, it was inevitable that much of what he did and planned would have to be done on his own initiative and without consulting his helpers, they for the most part being concerned with one aspect of the picture, he with the whole. This caused some unhappiness and even a loss of confidence among some of his more enthusiastic supporters; for his exceptional capacity for evoking loyalty could also boomerang into disillusionment when they found that he had only given to them a small part of his many-sided personality. This is true today, nearly ten years later, and will no doubt be so right up to the end.

CHAPTER FOUR

STAUNTON HAROLD

THE NEXT HOME was Staunton Harold, a historic but dilapidated mansion lying in a deep fold of beautiful countryside in Leicestershire. There is a place on the Ashby-Melbourne Road where you can scramble up the bank, and there a mile away on the far side of the lake is the house, in its eighteenth-century landscape. From this distance, at the time of which I am writing, the house would have looked much as it had done through the centuries; but in fact, after wartime requisitioning by the Ministry of Works, and occupation at various times during the war by Italian prisoners of war and British troops, it was an uninhabitable shell. When the Ministry of Works handed it back to Lord Ferrers, the owner, after the war, an enormous amount of money would have been needed to restore it, and the sum offered for this purpose was only about a third of what was necessary.

Lord Ferrers, whose ancestors, the Shirley family, had lived at Staunton Harold since before the Civil War, had suffered since childhood from the effects of poliomyelitis. He was loved and admired by the local people, and the house was part of the countryside and their lives. Now he and his family were living in the dower house, while the big house remained empty. Gradually the exterior deteriorated as well as the interior; great holes appeared in the roof, in winter the rain and snow poured down the staircase, and there was dry rot in the roof timbers.

Lord Ferrers tried without success to find an organization which might be willing to restore the Hall and then use it. Finally, he had to take the terrible decision: there was no alternative but to sell. The fabric was put up to auction, and the successful bid was made by a firm of house-breakers. On the day before the auction Lord Ferrers died.

Some time before, in 1952, Cheshire had met Lord and Lady Ferrers when they were staying in Cornwall. St. Teresa's, in the deserted hut on the Lizard, was already in action, with a few patients, and Cheshire invited the Ferrers family over there for tea. They had been deeply impressed, and later Cheshire was told by their secretary, Margot Mason, that Lord Ferrers had debated the possibility of offering him Staunton Harold for a Home, but had hesitated for fear of landing him with such a liability. He had in fact told his wife, after the meeting in Cornwall, that he felt Cheshire would exert a spiritual influence on the whole of their country-side if he should be inspired to take on Staunton—but the request would have to come from Cheshire himself.

Cheshire heard about the sale of Staunton Harold, and Lord Ferrers' death, while he was still at Midhurst, and soon afterwards Lady Ferrers sent him some of her late husband's clothes. He wrote back at once asking if there was any way in which the house could be saved. Could it, for instance, become a home for disabled people? She asked him if he could come and see for himself. He said he would.

It was a very cold day early in 1955, soon after he had left Midhurst. Snow was melting on the roof and pouring through the gaping holes into the big hall with its stone floor. Everywhere there was desolation and decay. Yet there was something else, too, which Cheshire noted. Lady Ferrers was not well, so he was shown round by Margot Mason and some others who knew the house, and he felt that they all had a real love for it.

They went first into the chapel, which had been

handed over to the National Trust in 1953. It had been built by an ancestor of Lord Ferrers in 1653, and was in fact one of the only two churches to have been erected in the time of Cromwell. Sir Robert Shirley was a brave man, for he built his private church at a time when Cromwell had forbidden all new ecclesiastical building, and the price of his disobedience was imprisonment and death in the Tower of London. In the chapel, Cheshire told Margot Mason he could feel love and peace everywhere about him, and when they went over the house he had this feeling even more strongly. After they had finished he said, "We must get this house somehow, and start a Home in it."

He asked Margot Mason if she could help him to get it back from the demolition contractor who had bought it at the auction. Fortunately, a six months' preservation order had been put on the property by the Government, on the advice of the Historic Buildings Council. If anyone should come forward during this time who was prepared to put it in order and use it for a good purpose, the demolition firm could be compelled to sell. But the matter would have to come before a Court of Enquiry, and if this Court decided in favour of the demolition firm, nothing could be done.

A Court of Enquiry was duly held in Ashby de la Zouche. In the course of it, the contractor sought to prove that it would be impossible to make the derelict house habitable. He showed photographs of holes in the roof and dry rot in the timbers, and produced a Ministry of Works estimate that £110,000 would be required to restore it. But Lady Ferrers and her family and the indomitable Margot Mason argued passionately that Group Captain Cheshire would be able to rescue the house and convert it into a home for the disabled. They won the case.

But now Cheshire had to set about finding the money —nearly sixteen thousand pounds; and this would give him only the house—a ruined stately home. He appealed to the Historic Buildings Council, but to his surprise they were not at all sympathetic towards his plan: the National Trust, they told him, was the only body fitted to look after such a house as Staunton Harold in a proper fashion. Cheshire was bitterly disappointed, because on top of everything else there was a time limit on the stay order issued by the Court of Enquiry. If he couldn't raise the money by the due date, the bulldozers would move in.

Cheshire managed to raise a little money from friends in London, and then the most extraordinary thing happened—by a strange coincidence, on the day when the Queen Mother was to pay an official visit to Le Court.

This is how Margot Mason described the scene: "We were there at Le Court lining up to meet her. I remember coming down the slope to the house with Lady Ferrers. Leonard was standing at the door shaking hands with everyone as they came along. He was holding a partly opened parcel in his left hand."

Cheshire welcomed Lady Ferrers, and then drew Margot Mason aside and gave her the parcel. "Here, Dopey, go and see what's inside this and count it, please. Better get into some unoccupied corner of a room before you open it all up."

(Dopey was the name given to Margot by the Shirley family because, like the seventh Disney dwarf, she is short and very active.)

She took the parcel into a corner, and found inside it a woollen jersey. Inside the jersey was a sugar carton stuffed with one-pound notes.

"I counted them: there were five hundred. Leonard came round with the Queen Mother. When he drew level with me he asked for the sugar carton and said to her: 'Look, Ma'am, what we've been given.' She looked mystified, and he said: 'Look inside, Ma'am.' When she did, and I said there was five hundred pounds in it, all in one pound notes, they both gasped."

Two days later a similar parcel, also with five hundred pounds inside, turned up. They found out later that the two parcels had come from an old lady who was going blind and had heard about Le Court and St. Teresa's.

Meanwhile, Cheshire had turned to private benefactors in a concentrated effort to find the big sum of money needed for Staunton Harold. One of the people he approached was George Ravenshear, who had made a fortune out of property dealing. The two men had met at Le Court in this first summer of Cheshire's freedom, and he had told Mr. Ravenshear the story of Staunton Harold. There were only a few days left before the deadline. Mr. Ravenshear made up his mind quickly. He promised five thousand pounds. Half an hour after making this decision he motored up to London from Littlehampton with a Wing Commander who had already interested him in the possibility of starting a Cheshire Home at Angmering in Sussex. By the time they reached London the five thousand had become ten thousand. Staunton Harold was saved.

There had been some local publicity in Leicestershire and Derbyshire as a result of the Court of Enquiry. So when the local people discovered that their help was welcome in getting some of the rooms at Staunton ready for Cheshire's first visit after the purchase, they came along enthusiastically with buckets and mops to scrub the floors and clear up the mess in the main ground-floor rooms. Reporters came along too, from Leicester, Nottingham and Derby, to photograph the Countess in her overalls mopping up the stone floors in the hall of what had once been her own house. Lady Ferrers would allow nobody to take her picture until they had done their own bit with bucket and mop. The enthusiasm grew when it was realized that every offer to help was being accepted; that, in fact, nothing could be done unless people did offer to help, for there was no money left after the demolition firm had been paid off.

Cheshire and the house had lit a spark in Leicestershire. Support groups were formed in neighbouring villages and in some of the industrial towns; but more important than the money, and even more effective, were the volunteers who poured into the house every week-end, and some even during the week. Margot Mason told me later:

"I well remember the first Sunday afternoon after Leonard's arrival. He had come in the bus. Hundreds of people came too, mostly in cars. Some of them took on one room, others another; organizations such as Rotary, the Round Table, Toc H, and so on, each took a room. They would lock the door of their room behind them when they left for the day so that others couldn't muscle in on their territory. There was tremendous rivalry."

At a time when there was some industrial unrest in the Midlands and strikes all over the country, a local quarry offered to re-do the drive. The employer gave the tarmac —120 tons of it—and the men gave their time, working through two week-ends from seven in the morning to nine at night. Because of the difficulties of transport some of them had to be up by two in the morning in order to get to the quarry and have the tarmac heated and loaded on the lorries, in time for the arrival of the working party.

And the big firms in the Midlands helped too, so that there could be a lift to the first floor with room in it for two wheelchairs. This opened up the whole of the first floor. In addition the entire house had to be re-wired, central heating had to be installed, and main water brought in from a mile away. Another thing which had to be done before the patients could come in was the installation of bathrooms, sluices, and so on. The first patient was installed within a few weeks, while all this work was going on.

The first matron was Miss Burton, known as "Barty," who has worked devotedly for the Cheshire Homes, in India as well as in England. She remembers vividly the early days at Staunton Harold. The big old house was still far from ready from any practical point of view, but the first few patients were touchingly happy to be there, and the Home was filled with an atmosphere of life and contentment—although there was no electricity, many of the ceilings leaked, much of the glass was missing, and there was only an aged broken-down Aga in the kitchen. The single room which was habitable was the very large stone-flagged entrance hall, and for the first two nights the patients lived and slept there.

To write of those who came to Staunton Harold is to describe in microcosm the wonderful spirit of the men and women who find a new life in the Cheshire Homes, and to whom, on the other hand, an undreamt-of chance of usefulness and happiness is offered. There is May, for instance, who was born a spastic, and had to live with distant relatives. They treated her with great unkindness, leaving her outside in a chair for hours on end, and finally even threatening her with an axe. Through Toc H she found refuge at Staunton. And Charlie Bolton, who all his life had been pushed around, living in workhouses and casual wards. Until he went to Staunton Harold he had never known what it was to be wanted or to have a home. Now, large and cheerfully unsteady on his legs, for the first time he is something more than just another mouth to feed.

Tom Gair had had to spend 4½ years in the geriatric hospital, where the other patients were many years older than he was, with the majority suffering from senile decay and literally just waiting for death. He had nothing in common with these men, and the prospect of having to end his days there terrified him. Then he came to Staunton, and found friends of his own age and interests. Here he can take an active part in the social life of the Home—every year he writes the script for the pantomime—and feel that he is a human being again, that he can live instead of simply existing.

Bill Bull, a shoemaker, had lived a very full life in the social and welfare fields, until his disability curtailed his work. He came to Staunton feeling that he was being put on the scrap-heap, but found instead that he had a big part to play, not only in helping to organize the social activities, but also in the reorganization of the occupational therapy side of the Home. He was largely instrumental in forming the very active branch of Toc H which now flourishes there, and his influence in this movement has spread beyond the four walls of the Home and left its mark on branches throughout the district. Bill sums up what Staunton has meant to him in these words: "I came to the Home thinking that my active life was over, but I soon found that another one was just beginning—and I enjoy every minute of it."

Finally, George Barnes, who is blind and chair-borne. Life in hospital would be dull and meaningless beyond words for him, but at Staunton he is able to take more than his fair share in everything that goes on. His work on the Patients' Committee is a valuable contribution towards the running of the Home; he takes a very active part in Toc H; and he is one of the stars of the pantomime team.

It was not until the Historic Buildings Council began to appreciate what Staunton Harold meant to the people of Leicestershire, what sacrifices they were willing to make, and how generous the contribution would be from many local firms and businesses, large and small, that they started to feel the Cheshire solution might work. When they did so it was agreed that the compensation money should be made available to restore the house as an architectural monument, and the compensation for war damage and the grant from the Council produced the sum of £30,000 which was needed. Cheshire felt that the money was grudgingly given, but certainly the house could never have been fully restored—as it is now—without it, and at least the story had a happy ending.

The rescue of Staunton Harold has always seemed to me to be the most daunting of Cheshire's many enterprises. Whatever the reason, the story has always stirred me deeply. The spirit of a house and of a family, the death of a brave man—these had been the things which had called Cheshire from the Sanatorium at Midhurst to the Midlands to start his fifth Home.

Over the west door of the chapel at Staunton Harold is an inscription to the memory of the courageous man who built it:

"In the yeare 1653
when all thinges Sacred were throughout ye nation
Either demolisht or profaned
Sir Robert Shirley, Barronet,
Founded this church;
Whose singular praise it is,
to haue done the best things in ye worst times,
and
hoped them in the most callamitous."

CHAPTER FIVE

AMPTHILL

On December 8th, 1954, Cheshire had left Midhurst apparently cured, although he was drastically curtailed in what he was allowed to do. He had converted one of the thirty-seater buses he had been given into an office-cum-bedroom, a house on wheels, so to speak, in which he could take his statutory two-hour daily rest, keep up his correspondence, even eat his meals as he travelled from one Home to another. With him, in her own car, went Margot Mason, whose work with the Shirley family had come to an end with the death of Lord Ferrers, and who had decided to throw in her lot—without salary—with Cheshire's venture.

The period which followed was a shaky one, a mixture of good and bad, a time when the impulse to surge forward was to clash with the call for consolidation and prudence from his helpers. In Cheshire's own mind, however, his vocation was at last clear: it was to found Homes wherever need or opportunity should demand, and for this he wanted to be equipped and ready. But whereas in the past he had been responsible only to himself, and could do more or less as he pleased, now he was working mainly through other people. At times he was to forget this, to take decisions on his own initiative that properly belonged to a local committee, or that would perhaps saddle a committee with responsibilities which they were not willing to accept.

From Midhurst he went to Parkminster, the Carthusian monastery, for a week's retreat, and then to his parents until after Christmas. During this period a letter came from an advanced incurable T.B. who could find nowhere to go other than expensive private nursing-homes, and who appealed for help. Cheshire was warned by the doctors that T.B. would soon cease to be a problem, and that there was no call for a Home for incurable cases, but he was unimpressed and vowed to do something about it. So he went to see Ampthill Park house, which belonged to Bovril's, and about which he had received a letter from the Historic Buildings Council. Had he known that the Council had sent precisely the same letter to a hundred or so other potentially interested parties he would probably never have gone, for his thoughts ran towards small premises in which he could gain a foothold and gradually advance, not towards large and derelict historic buildings. But he was so astounded that the Ministry of Works should think he might be a suitable user of the property that he went, his mind made up in advance.

Bovril's received him kindly in one of the small nucleus of rooms which they had preserved intact from the utter ruin of the rest of the once beautiful house; and, though they cannot have seriously thought that he would succeed in bringing Ampthill back into habitation with no resources behind him, they offered to give it to him as an outright gift if after due reflection he really wanted it.

While he had been in the sanatorium at Midhurst an Australian author had written a breezy biography dealing mainly with Cheshire's career in the Air Force and the beginning of his first two Homes. Subsequently the author of this book had introduced him to an Australian girl, Phil Loneragan, who decided to give up her holiday in Europe to become his secretary. She had means of her own, and not only did she accept no money at all, but she contributed many of the early secretarial expenses out of her own pocket. She also succeeded in finding a small London office, a converted corridor in a ground-floor mews cottage between Park Lane and Piccadilly. Into this one morning walked a man who introduced himself as Paul Latham, said that he didn't feel he'd made much of his life, and wondered if there was anything he could do to help. Phil, one of whose mottoes is "Never know till you ask," said that they urgently needed the loan of £1,000, and Cheshire, when told of Latham's offer of help, asked if he would go to Ampthill and prepare the house for his own arrival in ten days' time. The answer was one of the most surprising that can ever have come into the Foundation: "I didn't expect to be asked for money, but here is what you want. I wasn't planning on leaving home, but I'll go up there with two servants and see what I can do."

Paul Latham, as it turned out, was a baronet who had once been immensely wealthy, had had a domestic tragedy, followed a downhill path and finally served a sentence in jail. He was now catapulted into totally unfamiliar surroundings. Ampthill, other than the few ground-floor rooms which Bovril's had preserved and which were centrally heated, was cold beyond description, with a damaged roof, nearly half its window-panes missing, obsolete and scanty plumbing and no furniture. The helpers whom Latham was sent were all people who had problems of their own and were seeking some means of working them out of their systems. The sister-in-charge retired to bed on the evening of her arrival, and after a fortnight of being cared for by those who were already overworked themselves was declared unfit for work. The architect was told that £400 was the total sum available for essential repairs, and was asked to spend up to that amount to bring the maximum of rooms into use; he promptly put four times that value of work in hand without consulting either Latham or Cheshire. Worst of all, the T.B. patients, who were not tardy in coming, were by virtue of their disease incapable of doing anything to help themselves or the household.

Latham himself did little but throw cold water on the whole scheme. He said that he had had as much experience of historic buildings as most people, that this one would cost a fortune to run, quite apart from the fact that it had to be made habitable first, that by a terrific effort it might just be possible to get the place more or less going, but that it was doomed to failure in the end. Get out, find a new and more economical building, organize it on proper lines and start all over again, he said. But for all his doubts and grumbles he threw himself into it heart and soul. He financed the weekly maintenance costs out of his own pocket, brought up two pantechnicon loads of furniture, and spent hours of his time keeping peace among the helpers and trying to sort out their personal problems.

He didn't begin, however, to comprehend Cheshire's policy of accepting everything and anything that came, whether it was patients or helpers or gifts. When the Vicar called one day, to find out what was going on, and discovered that some of the household were reduced to sleeping on mattresses on the floor, he offered what he described as a rusty but still usable bed. The obviously affluent, mystifying man before him made a gesture of impatience, and said he really didn't think such a thing would be suitable at all. The Vicar retired crestfallen and even more puzzled than when he came. But when Cheshire pointed out to Latham that he had been wrong in refusing the bed—that whatever was offered, even if it were utterly useless and only a nuisance, one must look as if it were the thing one wanted most in the world—Latham drove straight off to the Vicar and told him the circumstances had now changed and there was nothing he needed more than that old bed, if it was still available. The Vicar was so delighted that he gave not only the bed, but much else besides.

Gradually the house was cleaned up, order emerged from disorder and a community life began to take shape.

All this imposed a great strain on Latham, whose life hitherto had been a very different one, passed within the walls of stately homes, certainly, but not of the kind he was now living and working in under conditions of considerable physical and climatic discomfort.

Cheshire has told me since that he can remember Latham sleeping in one of the upstairs bedrooms, where the windows had lost most of their panes, buried beneath two voluminous silk eiderdowns he had brought with him from his own house. He used to wind himself into them until it looked as if he was lying in a satin sleeping-bag. Then one day he developed a sore throat which soon got worse and was diagnosed as cancer. He would not recover. But he stuck to the house and to his self-appointed task almost until the end, and Sydney, his servant, stayed with him until he died. Before he died he told Cheshire that his last few weeks had been the happiest of his whole life.

Gradually the pattern of Cheshire's future methods was emerging. It was beginning to become clear to others beside himself that he had by chance lighted on a real need, and one which the National Health Service simply was not meeting. An increasing number of letters began to arrive at the London office, many of which Phil Loneragan forwarded on to him as he moved round the country, for it was clearly important for him to be in constant touch with the new Homes and to continue the search for more buildings in which to expand. But it was also necessary for him to have a fixed base, and this he entrusted to Phil. He was determined that the office in the mews cottage should not develop into a large headquarters which might swallow up his slender resources, and obscure his objective beneath a mass of paper and appeals. This clearsightedness has kept his growing movement on the narrow path towards his goal, that goal which can never be reached until all suffering has departed from the world.

It was during this summer of 1955, as he drove from one Home to another with Margot Mason and their mobile office, that a second biography appeared, bringing Cheshire's story up to the end of the war. It was a conscientious and painstaking work, which revealed much of his many-sided and complex personality. Both this book and the war story by the Australian writer hinted at the new life on which their subject was embarking, but they could do no more than sketch in the outline of the future as seen at the time when he had gone to Midhurst; their publication did, however, bring Cheshire's name back into the news at a time when his illness had caused it to be forgotten. One of the results was that the B.B.C. devoted an important programme by its outside TV camera unit to the new Le Court. This programme had two results: it introduced the Homes to the British public, and brought in a considerable amount of money in donations.

It may seem strange that Cheshire needed a dual headquarters—his Bedford bus and the mews office—particularly in view of his insistence on action and his distaste for paper-work. But, like most successful leaders, he understood that you cannot completely dispense with paper; but at the same time that there are two ways of handling it—you can either make it work for you or you can let it make you work for it. He knew that at any rate for some time to come, in the absence of his immediate presence, his personality and inspiration would somehow have to keep up the momentum of his movement. He could only be in one place at a time and there were only the twenty-four hours available, nearly half of which were bespoken for the rest on which his doctors firmly insisted. So there had to be letters and messages, there had to be these two devoted and efficient secretaries, both of whom were voluntary workers.

And then, in addition to the four Homes already in existence—Le Court, St. Teresa's, St. Cecilia's and

Ampthill—and the two that were coming along—Staunton Harold and St. Bridget's at Angmering—there was a small world of private and religious interests which did not come within the scope of the Homes. These activities, of which we have already seen a little, were grouped together for administrative and financial convenience in what he called the Mission for the Relief of Suffering. This enterprise consisted of a cheque-book operated by Phil and a tenuous account with a bank in Curzon Street, into which any money was paid that was handed to him personally without specific instructions as to how or where it should be spent.

One thing to which he devoted much of his time and which, as we have seen, he regarded as of major importance in his mission to the sick was the Holy Shroud of Turin, traditionally considered to be the winding sheet in which Christ had been buried. In March he addressed a crowded meeting at the Seymour Hall in London on this theme, and about the same time a full-page article appeared in the *Daily Mirror*, followed by an even longer one in *Picture Post*. This publicity added to the continuing activities of the bus, and aroused a great deal of interest.

In May he received a letter from the mother of a ten-year-old girl dying of osteo-myelitis, who was apparently convinced that if only she could touch a portion of the Shroud would she recover. When she received by return of post not a piece of Shroud itself—for that was physically impossible—but a reproduction of the majestic and inspiring face which the Shroud reveals when it is photographed, she astounded the doctors by sitting up in bed and saying that she wanted to get up and have an ice-cream. For three days she had eaten nothing at all, and the hospital had given up hope that she would ever eat again. Ten days later, when he was in the neighbourhood, Cheshire called to see her and to hear the story from her own lips. She was out of danger and at home with her parents—though still unable to walk by virtue of the deformity in her leg and hip—but her yearning to see and touch the Shroud was as strong as ever. It was explained to her that the Shroud was the property of the Royal House of Italy and securely locked away behind seven seals, only being brought out for public viewing and veneration once every fifty years or so; that many people had appealed to see it in vain; that in any case it was not the Shroud itself that was so moving and striking but the image revealed by photography, which could not be seen properly with the naked eye. Nevertheless, she was unmoved, saying that if only she could touch it she would walk again. When pressed as to why exactly she wanted to see it rather than the photograph, she answered: "Because I want to be blessed by it."

So, with the warm consent of her parents, the doctor and the Bishop, Cheshire disappeared with her on a lone and extraordinary journey across Europe, first to Lisbon to see King Umberto in exile, who was the legal owner of the Shroud, and then to Turin itself, where an astonished Cardinal broke the unwritten law and in the presence of all the many custodians, whom he was obliged hastily to summon, brought the Shroud from its casket for Josie to touch. Josie was not instantly cured, as she was firmly convinced she would be, but from that moment on she was at peace and reconciled with her disability. In the train on the way back to London she said: "I do wish the Shroud could be kept for everyone who wanted to see it. Then great honour would be done to our Lord." It was a remarkable statement for a girl of ten who had just had her hopes disappointed, and perhaps helps to vindicate Cheshire's claim that the Holy Shroud, by virtue of the light that it shines on the whole mystery of suffering, gives a new strength and sense of purpose both to those who suffer themselves and those who seek to help them.

A number of discharged prisoners were appealing to Cheshire for help at this time. Indeed, it seemed to him they had been doing so intermittently from the very beginning, which had been one of his reasons for setting up Holy Cross in Cornwall as a specialized unit where he could take them in. But this Home was now out of his hands, and not unnaturally the new committees of his latest Homes refused to have anything to do with such people. An opportunity seemed to offer itself for him to carry on this work during this busy summer of 1955, when the Historic Buildings Council came to him once more with a proposition that he should take on another of their architecturally important white elephants—for Cheshire had now become a potential user of stately homes, and figured prominently on their circulation lists. This time it was Wardour Castle, near Tisbury in Wiltshire. A large Palladian house, it had been the seat of the Arundel family for many generations and was built round a rotunda, its imposing public rooms opening off the circular space beneath the cupola. The family had not come back to the house after the war, and for a time it had been used as a college for the Roman Catholic priesthood, but the lack of heating and the dangerous state of the roof, and particularly of the ceilings of the public rooms, had caused them to abandon it. At this point someone in the Historic Buildings Council, desperate to find a user, persuaded Cheshire to take it on.

We had a talk about this episode many years later. I was particularly interested to hear the story and the intentions behind it, since one of the first decisions of the Trust in which I was called on to take part exactly one year later, when I had retired from India, was to be the closing down of Wardour Castle, and I was in fact to pay several visits to it, for we tried very hard to find some means of keeping it going. There had been little support from the people of the district, and now I can appreciate the reason, although at the time I don't think any of the Trustees had an inkling of the real motive behind Cheshire's acceptance of the enormous responsibilities represented by this derelict castle.

"My sole idea in taking Wardour," Cheshire told me, "was to have a place where we could rehabilitate gaol-birds by making them work for the sick. The idea had never been a popular one. In fact, from the moment the first committee was formed at Le Court I had been headed away from attempting anything of the sort. This was one of the reasons why I found it so difficult to give up my personal control. At Wardour, once it was known that this was my intention the opposition in the neighbourhood was fanatical. So much so that one of the most active helpers said he would never set foot in the Castle again. My difficulty was that the Trustees refused to concern themselves with anyone except the chronic sick, and yet objected to any other type of activity being publicly associated with my name. This meant that my only hope of doing other things at this period—like the gaolbirds, for instance—was by working entirely on my own anonymously without any organization or official support, and that obviously wouldn't last. At Wardour the very fact that I put the work in the hands of a committee placed them in an embarrassing position, and I was extremely sorry for this, when it worked out as it did. I could not approve the Trustees' decision to abandon Wardour, nor could I in good faith attempt to carry it on as a private venture."

The way in which Cheshire plunged into the experiment at this time is symptomatic of the period. The Trust was in its infancy, and in fact would not accept new Homes even of the conventional type until it was certain they were securely founded. The pattern of operating had not yet been firmly worked out, and Cheshire was becoming increasingly impatient with the new committees for not taking in either the heavier nursing cases or the unconventional and unusual helpers who seemed to him to be in as much need of succour as the physically handicapped; so he went on starting new Homes in the hope that the next committee would see eye to eye with him about these things. He had not yet appreciated that special types of cases, both physical and psychological, need specialized care from dedicated people. Another factor was that he was planning to leave England in the coming winter for India, and so he had to put the burden of his experiments on other people or else give them up altogether. In retrospect he admits that the failure of the Wardour experiment must be laid at his door. So far it is the only Cheshire Home in England that has had to be closed down.

Although Cheshire found that he was battering against a brick wall in trying to get the committees of Homes and indeed the Trustees themselves to look with any sort of favour on the unconventional side of his work, there was a new departure at this time from the developing pattern of the Homes which the Trustees were able to approve of, and for this he was thankful.

Barry Richards, a business-man from Kent, had recently joined the Trust. He was interested in problems of mental health. As a result of a year's investigation carried out at Cheshire's request by two helpers, we had a meeting one evening at Pitts Head Mews attended by three doctors from Belmont, the mental hospital in Surrey. This meeting turned out to be the opening of a door on to a whole new field of work among the handicapped, and Cheshire was delighted to find that it was one of the Trustees who was apparently pointing the way. It was a stony field which did not appeal very much to the many people who were coming forward now to work for the physically disabled. To Cheshire, as with the gaolbirds, the social misfits and the maladjusted presented a challenge.

In the early years of Le Court he had tried to take in

a number of the same kind of people as the Belmont doctors described to us—those who had been discharged from mental hospitals and who, because of the absence of a stable home background, were finding it difficult to adapt themselves to normal living. This experiment had been only partially successful, and once the first committee came into existence and took charge of Le Court this type of helper-patient was not acceptable. The idea put to us by Barry Richards and the doctors of Belmont suggested a possible solution which might be more professional and capable of control than the haphazard methods of his early days, and so recommend itself to the more cautious outlook of his Trustees. The doctors were asking, in effect, if he could start a Home which would be a hostel, a temporary resting-place for some of these discharged mental patients, many of whom were breaking down under the stress and strain of their initial return to the outside world.

One of the phrases used by these doctors was very graphic, and put the problem in a nutshell: "It's like extinguishing a burning log and then throwing it back into the fire."

Far too many people, they said, who leave mental hospitals do not have a family, or at any rate not a sympathetic one to whom they can go to regain their confidence. These people rarely have the resilience to stand on their own feet the moment they leave the shelter of the hospital.

When Cheshire was told of this request he at once grasped its significance—the need for a comfortable and sympathetic Home to which they could return after work, for they must work in order to re-establish themselves in society. Their stay would not be permanent, but would be a stage in their rehabilitation. If they could not work, then they could not stay. It would be the first time Cheshire had ever tackled anything on these lines, and certainly the first time he could see himself doing anything unconventional in a controlled and approved manner.

A house was found in Wimbledon. Cheshire called it Miraflores. Although there were difficulties and mistakes, it soon established itself on a permanent footing, thanks in considerable measure to the enthusiasm of Barry Richards, who in due course, with his hard-working committee, bought the house next door to provide additional accommodation of this specialized nature—the beginning, it is to be hoped, of much more of the same kind. Indeed, it would not be long before there would be a Home for mentally handicapped children in Dorchester. But this, too, required a long and difficult struggle by a handful of devoted people before it was firmly established.

The 20th of April of this year, 1955, when the Queen Mother had visited the new Le Court, had been another milestone. The gathering of people from Cornwall, from St. Cecilia's, St. Bridget's and Ampthill, and a few from Leicestershire, as well as the Trustees, who came to be presented to the Royal guest and to make friends with the patients, staff and helpers at Le Court, had given Cheshire the idea of perpetuating this coming together of his growing family of friends and helpers. From that day on, with the Queen Mother's full approval, Family Day, held in rotation in the different Homes, has become an annual feature of the movement.

Cheshire's decision to go to India had been taken in the Midhurst sanatorium at a time when there were only two Homes in England, and when he had been making no particular effort to start any more. A tea-planter from the Annamallai Hills in south India had written to him telling of the very great need in India for the sort of Homes he was bringing into existence in England. This man came on home leave while Cheshire was in Midhurst, and went to see him. Cheshire's mother and father and Phil Loneragan were the only people who knew of his decision at that time, and it was kept a well-guarded secret for many months—in fact, for most of this summer of 1955. But when it came to the time for making plans, inevitably the news got out.

At first most people refused to believe that the young man whom they had followed to such remarkable successes in different parts of the country could seriously be planning to abandon them. It was the same reaction on a larger scale as that of the patients and staff at Le Court when they had first learned of his plan to start St. Teresa's. I think the Cornwall episode had carried its lesson for him too. Then he had taken a calculated risk that the second venture might destroy the morale of those whom he had left behind to consolidate the initial success of the first. His absence had compelled them to struggle, and by doing so had proved to them that his personal presence was not indispensable, that the work would go on if there was faith. Moreover, it had given them a sense of personal achievement, of identity with their own particular Home which they would never have had if he had been continually there himself. Why, therefore, should he not take one further step still and go abroad, always providing that he was responding to a need and not acting on his own initiative? The call in this case had come from India, a country he scarcely knew and had only visited once briefly, towards the end of the war, when it had not especially attracted him. But the summons was genuine and urgent, and to turn his back on it would be to depart from his fundamental principles.

Nevertheless, the consternation was all the greater now than it had been at Le Court, because the field of his endeavours had become so much wider. And the many who were critical and afraid were able to point out that the country he had chosen for the continuance of his work had but recently become independent of

British rule. Surely the Indians would not want any Britishers back so soon after they had become free? He explained his decision to me the following spring, a few days after I had come back to England for good after twenty-one years in business in India.

"There are some calls that ring clear and true. This was one of them. I did nothing to encourage Bob to start St. Cecilia's, yet he came back and back. To have refused would have been equivalent to refusing Arthur Dykes. The call from India seemed to have the same kind of ring; it was so compelling that I should have been doing wrong to ignore it. Even though the odds seemed heavily against living up to the promise, I felt an inner conviction that it was right to make it. But there was another factor too.

"On my previous visit to India during the war I didn't come into contact with the ordinary people, though I know I should have done. But I came away with the impression that England had gone to India more with a view to what it could take out than what it could put in. I don't mean to belittle what we did and gave in the field of administration and engineering and that sort of thing, but I don't really believe we did what we might have done for the poor and the helpless."

He paused for a moment. He wasn't often serious in conversation, and so often pulled people's legs with his solemn remarks made with a poker face that I was never altogether certain when he was being serious and when not. But there was no doubt about his seriousness now.

"I always think that it's the responsibility of every nation to pass on to others what it has learnt. I consider that what made Britain a great country was her willingness to go to other people's help even to her own detriment, and I recognize no other criterion of greatness. Now that we have given India her independence there is double reason for offering help because we stand nothing to gain. Help that is given for an ulterior motive is not help at all."

"Yes; that's quite true. I can see that. But what about your Homes here?" I had asked him.

"They can't be much good, can they, if they have to have me around all the time? If they can't do without me, then I shall have failed them. Secondly, and perhaps more fundamentally, is the necessity for all of us to be outward, not inward, looking. It is on this, to my mind, that everything hinges. For if we are to succeed then all of us, those who are helped and those who help, must have their eyes fixed outside themselves. The day that any single part of the Foundation thinks it has achieved its goal and can really carry on just maintaining its position, it has lost its direction and its life. That's really why I had to answer the call from India."

The summer of 1955 was now well on its way out. Staunton Harold had admitted its first patients and was evoking a much greater response from the people of the Midlands than Ampthill was from Bedfordshire, where the death of Paul Latham had deprived it of its inspiration and administrative cohesion. Cheshire came to the rescue by deciding to mount his expedition to India from Ampthill. He set up his headquarters by the main entrance, and was able both to supervise the plans for the trip and to take the place of the gallant man who had given the last months of his life to this rambling and inefficient house.

His original idea was that four of them should travel overland to India in the bus and a landrover which he had been given. Apart from himself the expedition was to consist of Margot Mason, whose headquarters was now established in one of the bedrooms at Ampthill; Sydney, one of Latham's servants, who had stayed on after the death of his master; and Roy, who had been travelling round with Cheshire throughout the summer in the bus and was the engineer of the party. Shortly before they were due to leave, Cheshire decided that it would be more practical for the other three to go by sea, while he flew out ahead to prepare the ground in Bombay, their first port of call. Rather casually, and certainly most unfortunately, they decided to take the two vehicles on the usual form of triptyque, the international document which is the normal administrative form carried by motorists touring on the Continent. A well-known shipping company generously agreed to carry the vehicles free on the deck of one of their cargo vessels, and to take the three sea-borne members of the expedition for a nominal sum.

Then the day came for them to go. First Cheshire, then the rest of them. Ampthill Park House, where the emptiness and the sadness caused by the death of Paul Latham had been temporarily overlaid by the bustle and excitement of the expedition, found itself alone. The gracious eighteenth-century house set on its hillside above the rolling Bedfordshire countryside was left with its T.B. patients, its struggling staff, and a handful of friends in the nearby market town. Cheshire was six thousand miles away, and the man who had carried the big house on his shoulders from the very beginning, around whom it had grown from a shell into a living thing, would never come back. They were left with their echoing corridors, the cold, historic rooms, and very little money. That Ampthill survived and flourished is a memorial to the man who had come to Cheshire with his tentative offer of help and his load of personal sorrow.

CHAPTER SIX

BETHLEHEM IN BOMBAY

AT THIS STAGE I met Cheshire for the first time. I had heard of his exploits in Bomber Command, particularly the raid on Munich and his taking over 617 Squadron from Guy Gibson after the latter's death. Somewhere I had read about the Cheshire Homes, but I had only the haziest notion what they were. I suppose inevitably I had assumed they were something to do with ex-Servicemen. Then one day in December of 1955, when I was still living in India, I noticed a small paragraph in the *Times of India* with a photograph. The story referred to Cheshire's Victoria Cross and to his war record. It went on to say that he had arrived in India to start Homes for incurables and for the chronic sick. That was all.

It seemed the least likely thing that we should meet, since I had decided, reluctantly and after much heart-searching, to leave India ten years sooner than would have been normal for an English business-man. My wife and I were booked to sail in the *Himalaya* from Bombay in April of the following year. Already we were pulling up our roots one by one; for my wife this would be a difficult, painful business, for she was Indian and had never been abroad from India until we were married. For me it was quite different, since I should be returning to the country I had left as a young man twenty-one years before. The decision to cut short a career before its last and perhaps most interesting decade, with the corollary of starting again in England at forty-five, had not been easy; and for my wife it would mean a completely new life. Both our minds, therefore, were on other things that December morning. I supposed that I should never run into Cheshire; and the thought added to the regrets of that time.

Christmas came and went. One day early in January, on my way to the office, I dropped in to see my sister-in-law, who lived by the sea on the slopes of Malabar Hill. On that January morning she was sitting at her writing-desk. She was busy with one of the many charities in which she was involved.

"You must have a look at this correspondence."

She handed me a bunch of letters and sat me down at her desk. I could see out of the window across the lawns to the palm trees and the sea.

The letters told an extraordinary tale, the story of Margot Mason's arrival in Bombay a month before with the two young men and the bus and the landrover. I looked at the signature. It was that of Rajkumari Amrit Kaur, Health Minister in Mr. Nehru's Government. She insisted that she was writing as a friend, not in her official capacity, because obviously she could not interfere with the workings of the Indian Customs, however obstructive these might appear to be. Evidently she hoped that my sister-in-law, because of the great amount of work which she did for charity, might find a solution to the problem.

The difficulties would not have arisen if Cheshire had agreed to declare himself a tourist who had come to India with his bus and landrover to spend the winter. The triptyque was in order for that purpose. But he had insisted that he had come to India to establish, if he could, Homes for the sick. He had a letter from the Minister of Health as evidence of the Government's approval of the venture. But the Customs were bound by their regulations. If the two vehicles were to come into the country other than on a tourist basis, they must have an import licence. My heart sank. I knew just how long these documents took to come by. But I could see the point of the Customs. I also sensed for the first time Cheshire's uncompromising honesty, and I learned, too, of the extraordinary methods he used to get around the world, for somewhere in the correspondence it had said that he had only ninety pounds with him on arrival. The demurrage on the bus and landrover, which had been sitting in the docks for five weeks, already amounted to over a thousand pounds. Could something possibly be done about it, unofficially and quietly?

"What is Cheshire doing?" I asked my sister-in-law.

"He's living in the jungle out beyond Santa Cruz airport. He has bought some land—don't ask me how—and is building a Home for sick people. He has four patients already. But you had better meet Miss Mason, his secretary, who is staying at the Y.W.C.A. in town. She is handling this problem. We must do something to get the bus and landrover out of the Customs, as he can't really manage without them."

Something had to be done. As for Cheshire, he seemed too remote in his jungle, and without having met him I sensed that he had dropped the problem, confident that it would be solved by Providence. I 'phoned Miss Mason and we had lunch at the Taj, where she told me the whole story. She was less philosophical than Cheshire, for she knew the size of the bill for demurrage, which was growing every day the vehicles stayed in the docks uncleared.

Meeting Margot Mason gave me some idea of the sort of person Cheshire must be. She exuded cheerfulness and a gay, informal courage. India was a new and very strange experience for her, particularly as she was living in spartan and unfamiliar conditions at the Y.W.C.A., where there were no fans and the food was Indian style only. The voyage had been fun, but it had not been P. & O. first-class. And now at the very start there was all this trouble about their transport.

Their little party had been met by an Englishman and his half-Polish wife, Jimmy and Nina Carney, to whom they had their sole letter of introduction. This couple were to become instrumental in making Cheshire's inspiration immediately effective in Bombay.

Nina, the wife, had driven them from the docks to the great new oil refinery at Sewree which her husband managed. The journey took them through the heart of Bombay's congested dockland and its sprawling new industrial areas. None of them had been east of Suez in their lives. Margot Mason particularly was flabbergasted by what she saw during that first car drive from the ship—the crowds, the congestion, the poverty. For an English girl who had lived most of her life in the ordered peacefulness of the English countryside, it produced a severe emotional shock which almost knocked her out.

As we sat in the air-conditioned hotel dining-room, there was no sign of this shattering personal experience. All her thoughts were for the bus and landrover. From now on many of us worked on those vehicles, and appropriately it was my former service, the Indian Air Force, and an old friend of the war, Sobruto Mukerjee, now Chief of the Air Force, who prised them loose. We happened to run into each other just at the right moment, when he was paying a flying visit of inspection to Indian Air Force units in Bombay, and we went together to see the Chairman of the Port Trust. We also saw the Collector of Customs.

The Air Marshal said to the Government official: "I want those vehicles out of the Customs somehow."

"Well, I will let them out when I get the money." The Customs official shrugged his shoulders.

I looked at Sobruto and wondered what he would say.

"The Air Force will pay." The reply came quickly and clearly.

"Can you give me that in writing?"

"Of course."

The Air Marshal, who had been standing up until now, sat down at the table, pulled a Biro pen from an inner pocket, and wrote one sentence on a sheet of Customs notepaper.

The surprised Collector gave me a permit to take away the bus and landrover. And that was the last we ever heard of the matter.

Next morning, three weeks after the talk with my sister-in-law, Roy, Sydney and I pushed the petrol-less landrover through the Red Gate, the main exit from the Bombay Docks; and later in the afternoon Margot Mason and I drove out of the town to Bethlehem House, in the jungles of Salsette Island. In recent times this large island north of Bombay has begun to sprout with urban development, and its lovely jungles have been slowly pushed back by the spreading tentacles of the neighbouring industrial city. But in the middle, where the land rises in a line of gentle hills, it is still as much a part of rural India as you can find. We turned off the crowded main road at Andheri, crossed the railway line, and drove into the heart of the island. The crowds, which had been dense on the main road, thinned out as we left the suburbs behind us.

"This is where we turn off the macadam road," Margot Mason said. We crawled for a mile and a half through the jungle along the bullock track. Clouds of red dust rose from the wheels as we slithered over potholes and cart-ruts, and past village ponds, stagnant and filthy, but serene in the winter sunlight, until we turned off the track up a steep rise, past another board with its cheerful arrow, and emerged through a thicket into a clearing. There was an open space among the jungle trees. In the centre was an asbestos cement hut. At first I couldn't see any people about the place, but that was because we had come on the hut from the back. All the same, there was an atmosphere of movement and activity in the jungle clearing. Margot Mason took charge, for she knew the place and was clearly part of it in some way. I wondered what Cheshire would be like. Then, as we rounded the corner of the hut, I saw him for the first time. He was wearing grey flannels and an open-necked shirt, and was walking along the veranda of the hut carrying a bowl of water. He grinned, and said with deep seriousness:

"Hello, Dopey, we hadn't seen you for so long we thought you had gone back to England."

He seldom spoke in the first person singular, I discovered; I also found out to my cost that he was a past master at leg-pulling.

She blushed and laughed.

This was my first sight of Cheshire, and my first taste of the peculiar atmosphere he created around him.

"I must just finish doing Pop. Go into the office. I'll be with you in a minute."

He disappeared with bandages and hot water into the first compartment of the hut. We sat down on soap-boxes in the third room at the far end. There was a table, a recording machine, a shelf of books on theology, boxes full of medical stores, and a jumble of papers and oddments that reminded me of an R.A.F. Flight Commander's office in an operational unit.

Then Cheshire came in. Again there was the broad grin. Again I was struck by his slight build. He seemed to float through the air. I had read somewhere of his illness. He looked fit enough now. Margot Mason introduced us. He looked me straight in the eye and the playfulness disappeared for a moment.

"I can't thank you enough for what you did about the bus and landrover." Then the grin again. "Has Dopey told you what we're trying to do?"

He asked her to go into their immediate needs from Bombay with the two boys outside, while he talked with me. He told me of his methods.

"Most people think it's a bit crazy to take in patients before you have the roof on. I always think it's best to get your feet in the door, then it's easier to let the rest of your body in. We've got four patients here now, and this hut was only just finished the other day. An Indian contractor gave us the materials and built it free, and he has promised to put up a second one alongside, if we can get the materials."

"Have you got them yet?" I asked.

"Not yet; but I expect they will turn up some time. When they do we can bring nurses in. Then we can move on somewhere else and start a new Home."

I had never come across anything like this in my life, even in India, where the strangest things can happen. I had known nothing of his activities in England during the last few years, apart from the name "Cheshire Homes"; and somehow, in pursuit of the immediate aim of getting the bus and landrover out of the Customs, I had assumed that Cheshire in his jungle would be working for some time, probably a year or more, on getting one Home going. The idea that he was already planning to move on elsewhere, when he seemed to be at the very beginning of this project, took my breath away.

"Let's go round the estate." Again the grin.

There was not much to see then, yet there were a host of things. Two of the three rooms that gave off the veranda were occupied by the four patients.

"We've got a visitor to see you, Mr. Mesquita," Cheshire cried gaily to the corpse on the first bed. The face of skin and bones turned towards me. There was little life in the glazed eyes.

"He was brought in the other day. Not much time left to him, poor old chap, but he seems to be happy here. His family wanted to push him out. Pereira, the other chap, is a Goan cook. He can't speak—he's had a stroke—but I think he's happy."

There didn't seem much to be done about them, yet Cheshire had given them clean sheets, a clean bed and nursing from his own hands. I could imagine what their own homes had been like.

In the first room off the veranda there were no beds. Two Hindus, obviously of the poorest class, squatted on the floor.

"Pop, over there, was our first patient. He's our mascot. We don't understand a word he says and he can't cope with English, but Sydney and he get on as if they had known one another all their lives. He's a fine man; always keeps the room spotless and tries to help himself. He's got cancer of the groin, so he hasn't much time left, poor old boy, but he's happy and we love him."

The old Hindu sat cross-legged on the floor, a loin-cloth his only covering. He slid over the floor and tried to kiss Cheshire's feet.

"The fourth, Narayan, is an old rogue. I think he must have been a professional beggar. He escaped once and we had to fetch him back. He eats like a horse."

As we walked beneath the mango trees to the east, where you could see down through the jungle across the valley, Cheshire told me of his plans for his work in India and of how he operated.

"We go where we are asked to go, where the need is," and he spoke of the planter who had visited him in Midhurst. "This Home should be all right once we can get people interested. Nobody knows much about us yet, which is a good thing. Too much publicity at the start might not be so good. Sometimes you get landed with the wrong sort of people on committees, and it's difficult to shake them off."

I then asked the obvious question he had been asked so often in England. "How do you do for money?"

He grinned, more broadly than ever.

"You'd be surprised. It usually comes at the last minute, just when it looks as if everything is lost."

We had reached a shady place where the mango trees were thickest. There was an iron bedstead with a mosquito net over it, and a small bedside table with a prayer-book on it. We sat on the ground and Sydney brought us tea. Margot was busy at the other end of the little camp. I discovered that none of the party was being paid.

"Our road is pretty poor, isn't it?" He started talking again. "In the monsoon it will be impassable, a morass of mud. Something will have to be done to have an all-weather road."

This was expecting rather a lot, I thought, especially in the era of five-year plans. He went on to speak of his neighbour, a Buddhist monk from Ceylon, who lived in the Kanheri Caves, a mile further into the jungle. I remembered the caves well from my earlier days in Bombay, when I had sometimes ridden out to them through the grasslands for a picnic. Like all Buddhist monasteries of the earliest times, they were perfectly sited to achieve the maximum of privacy and peace. The view from these caves across the valley was very beautiful.

Cheshire continued: "I was so intrigued when I heard about him that I invited him to have a cup of tea. I wanted to find out something about him and his beliefs. He said, out of the blue, that he thought the Government ought to build a road so that pilgrims could come up and see his caves. They're very historic, but not many people know about them."

The first chairman of the management committee of the Home was an Indian who happened to be head of the Public Works Department. Cheshire told him about the monk's suggestion. He was enthusiastic about the idea, and put a survey team on to the job at once. When he had the estimate, four lakhs of rupees—thirty thousand pounds—he dropped the project like a hot brick.

The Manager of the oil refinery and his wife, Jimmy and Nina Carney, were the two people who got this first

Cheshire Home in India on to its feet. Cheshire had bought the land on a promise to its owner to pay when he could. The owner was glad to sell it at all. After that initial step, a friendly Indian building contractor, one of Jimmy's regulars from the refinery, had put up the first asbestos cement hut free, and soon the word got around Bombay, so that other business-men, Indian and British, were sending their lorries up the bullock-cart track with all the things the contractor needed for the second and third huts.

Jimmy sent a steamroller unit to make a tarred stretch of about 200 yards of roadway between the bullock track and the jungle clearing, and before we left for good in April he found a ten-thousand-gallon water tank, had it manhandled through the jungle, and connected it with improvised gutters on the roof of the huts, so that the Home could dispense with the daily visit of the bullock-drawn water-cart from the neighbouring convent.

Water was a serious problem. Nobody the committee consulted believed there could be water on top of a hill—and they had consulted a lot of people. Tired of the interminable and fruitless schemes which seemed to be getting nowhere, Jimmy threw the umpteenth contractor's report into his waste-paper basket and decided to make his own bore-hole on the site. He chose a one-man firm with an ancient drill powered by a two-stroke engine and set him to work. When the drill hit rock—at six feet—the man was for giving up. Jimmy was stern with him.

"All I want you to do," he said, "is to bore. Just bore. When I want you to stop, I'll tell you."

So the man bored from early February, 1957, until April, cutting through the Deccan trap-rock of western India with the General Manager of the large oil refinery sitting mercilessly on his neck. After three months, and at a greater depth than a drill of this size can have ever reached before, the man struck water, and disaster was averted, for in the monsoon, which breaks on Bombay in early June, the jungle would have become impassable, and the bullock-drawn water-cart could not have got through. Soon after water had been struck a load of piping appeared at the bottom of the two-mile track at its junction with the main road. It was the first evidence of official assistance, for the local municipality was going to put in main drainage.

But the Carneys' greatest contribution was undoubtedly finding the means of ensuring that the Home should be financially secure. Bethlehem House in Bombay has probably had fewer of those nagging financial worries which normally characterize the early days of a Cheshire Home than almost any other. At the first committee meeting under the mango trees, which took place against the background music of hammering and construction work, Nina had made her dramatic suggestion:

"I know. My husband will put on a pantomime."

Jimmy was a practical Yorkshire engineer. He had been sceptical of the whole idea when Cheshire had first arrived. Starting a hospital in rural India with no money and on top of a hill where there couldn't possibly be any water, and at the end of a bullock track which would be a torrent of slush in the monsoon—it had all seemed a crazy idea. But when he had become well and truly involved, and I suppose, too, because his great refinery, which had been erected in record time, was now smoothly turning crude oil into petroleum products, he seemed to find nothing incongruous in applying his energy to writing a script for a pantomime. It was duly put on in the lovely garden of a Parsee lady on Malabar Hill. From start to finish it was home-made—costumes, script and music. The success was so great that the single performance they had planned had to be extended to four. The Home received a cheque for the equivalent of three thousand pounds.

The Finance Minister of Bombay was so struck when he saw it that he asked Cheshire what he could do to help. Cheshire asked if the jungle track, all two miles of it, could be tarmacked.

I used to visit Bethlehem House in those exciting early days as often as I could, but the business of leave-taking after twenty-one years in Bombay made my time very scanty. There was, however, one incident which took place in Bombay and which I found of great interest. Cheshire had asked if he could meet Morarji Desai, the Chief Minister of Bombay. As we had been friends over the years, this was easy to arrange.

Morarji Desai was a controversial figure who ruled over Bombay State firmly and fairly, but because of his Gandhian views on alcohol and his ascetic ways he had acquired the reputation of being a sort of Hindu Oliver Cromwell. Some aspects of Bombay's Western-style, cosmopolitan social life had certainly suffered during his régime of prohibition. But he was a strong, fearless and capable ruler. We were ushered into his office in the brand new Secretariat building which he himself had planned and built, and, as always, I was struck by the contrast between the man and his surroundings—his simplicity of dress and manner and the modern setting of his office. The two men, who now met each other for the first time, had much in common, although they came from such different backgrounds. Cheshire wore a light suit, well cut; Morarji, as usual, was in *khaddar*, the homespun Indian cloth worn by all true followers of Mahatma Gandhi.

It was at this meeting that I heard, for the first time, how it all started.

Morarji was clearly interested in his visitor. This was for him a strange kind of Englishman, for he was not even a missionary.

"You were a man of war. Now you are a man of peace. What made you change?" Morarji was always direct.

"It was the sight of the atom bomb exploding on Nagasaki that made me really think about the purpose of life. I decided that I should like to help to see that such a bomb never had to be dropped again, for I felt that to win the war was not enough; one must also win the peace. But I started at the wrong end. I thought in terms of big plans and ambitious schemes. And I failed. Then I understood that to achieve anything lasting you must start from small beginnings, and build outwards; that the way to contribute towards the peace of the world is to bring peace into your own surroundings, into someone else's life—first, of course, into your own."

Morarji listened intently. Then he nodded his head and spoke at some length of Gandhi and renunciation. They talked for half an hour. They understood one another.

When we emerged from the Chief Minister's Office on the fifth floor of the building and reached the top of the stairs, Cheshire said to me suddenly: "Bet you I reach the bottom before you do."

I dashed for the top stair and careered down two steps at a time. When I got to the bottom, I was alone. Then I saw the lift doors open and out stepped Cheshire, roaring with laughter.

As soon as the transport was released from the Customs and put on the road, he left Bombay on a rapid tour of India. Margot Mason and the two young men stayed behind at Bethlehem House. On my last travels round India in the spring of 1956 I saw him several times, in Calcutta and in Delhi. He never seemed to have any money, yet he was the most mobile man in the country. He never asked for help, yet everyone wanted to help him.

We inspected a bungalow outside Calcutta on the Jessore road. I remember it well, as the instructions we had been given for finding it mentioned milestone 109.

"Not likely to forget that number," he laughed. "Saw too many of them in the war."

It was the only spontaneous reference I recall him making, then or later, to the war.

The second hut had been completed at Bethlehem House by the time Cheshire flew back to England in April, 1956, and work was started on a third. Some time before Cheshire had been able to come to an arrangement with a Spanish Order of Nuns which had recently come to work in India; the Mother Superior had agreed to provide a regular cadre of nursing sisters for the Home. This would be more satisfactory than the amateur attentions of Sydney and Roy, who, with Margot Mason, would be released to move to another part of the sub-continent to start another Home.

The Sisters of the Missionaries of Christ Jesus arrived at Bethlehem in the hot weather of 1956 and took over the staffing of the Home. Margot Mason and the young men then drove the landrover eleven hundred miles through central and northern India to Dehra Dun, at the foot of the Himalayas, in the great province of Uttar Pradesh. They were joined by a third young man, Michael, who had applied to Cheshire in England with an offer to help him abroad. Cheshire had accepted his offer partly because of his knowledge of Chinese, and partly in order to give him a new start in life.

None of them knew anything of India except for the little they had seen of Bombay, but their experiences at Bethlehem House had been of a kind which few Englishmen like myself, who thought we knew something about the country, had ever remotely known even during operations in the war. They had slept for three months in the open; their only connection with the outside world had been the occasional visitor from Bombay; until they got their transport, water had been hard to come by, their feeding had been precarious. There had been scarcely any money, and their companions had been four very sick old Indians whose language they didn't understand. So the long and dusty drive through Indore, Gwalior and central India to Delhi and on to Dehra Dun was not the ordeal it might otherwise have been. I have done that journey several times by car in the good season with comfortable rest-houses or the occasional hotel to relax in at the end of a tiring day's driving; the four of them had little money left over after paying for their petrol and one or two running repairs, and more than once were reduced to sleeping by the side of the road. This would not have seemed odd to our ancestors in India a hundred years ago, for they were used to hard living in the heat of India far from England; but most of us in 1956 had got so accustomed to our air-conditioning units and the many servants that I doubt if we could have accepted at all willingly the hardships which these four young people took in their stride, led by a girl whose first reaction to India's poverty and squalor had been one of horror and revulsion.

When they got to Dehra Dun they went straight to an empty palace in the cantonment area, which the Maharani of Nabha had already given to Cheshire. It had been the country house in this pleasant town—a sort of Indian Cheltenham, where many Government officials settle down in retirement—of the Maharajah, who had ruled over one of the Punjab Princely States, now merged, in the terminology of the times, with the neighbouring ex-British India. It was a typical Victorian wedding-cake house, ugly outside, with turrets and crenellations and a hint of Portuguese baroque; spacious inside, with large rooms and high ceilings. At the back was a wide courtyard with outhouses and servants' quarters.

Margot Mason surveyed it with an apprehensive eye. After Staunton Harold anything was good, perhaps, but here in India would one find the same voluntary helpers and the same response? For here was a house, smaller by far, it is true, but which had fallen into much the same state of disrepair. They began on the bees' and hornets' nests in the roof. Most of the ancient buildings in India, which are usually characterized by very high ceilings, become the home of great swarms of bees, which hang in dark clusters out of reach of human hands.

When they had got rid of these uncomfortable residents they started calling on the neighbours, who already had become not a little curious about the four young English people with their landrover who seemed to be sleeping on camp-beds in the deserted palace, living out of tins and attacking the many swarms of bees, and who didn't seem to fit into any pattern of English humanity they had yet seen.

The first call was on the English Headmaster of the Doon School, the Indian public school which had been started in 1935 and had been a most remarkable success. He stood high in the esteem of the Central Government and the State Government, and of Indians of all communities in Dehra Dun. He saw quickly what Cheshire was driving at. Then the usual stream of visitors and cars and helpers began to flow into the old Nabha Palace. In its small way, the story of Staunton was repeated. Only in one respect was it utterly different—there were no patients.

They simply would not come in. The committee had been prepared for any difficulty and obstacle in the world except this; and it nearly knocked them off their perch. The difficulty was partly that, as there was no almoner system in India, it was not easy for people to know that this new Home existed, nor indeed, if they should come to hear of its existence, that they would comprehend its purpose and the rather special kind of atmosphere and care which it was going to try to create for sick and disabled people. In India, where family ties are so strong among the poor, even if they are handicapped, there is always a fear of the unknown; and hospitals, which for people in the West instinctively conjure up pictures of care and of curative activities, in India sometimes, even among the better-off, mean institutions where they will be separated from their families, their friends and their familiar food.

Once they did begin to come in, and found that they could be visited at all times by their friends and relations, that the food was familiar and that the former palace was in fact an extension of their own home, they gained confidence. The news spread, and there was soon no shortage of patients.

The little team was disbanded. Margot was needed in England, Roy's father was calling him, and Sydney felt that it was time he earned his living again. Furthermore, the Indian Foundation, if it was to endure and grow, would have to stand on its own feet. Sydney got a job in Calcutta, Margot Mason and Roy came back by sea to England, which they had left eight months before, and Michael moved on to a job at an Australian university. As newcomers to the East they had achieved a lot in a short space of time. Behind them they left, in Dehra Dun, the nucleus of what was to develop into one of the most significant aspects of Cheshire's work.

CHAPTER SEVEN

THE RED FEATHER

Early during Cheshire's time in India he had received two letters by the same post, both from South India—one from the widow of an Indian Government official, a Mrs. Chinnadorai, and the other from Michael, a schoolmaster who said he was suffering fiom "shaky pollisie." Michael's letter was a most urgent and desperate appeal for help. "Please take me at all costs," he wrote. He sent the letter through the Archbishop of Madura, who forwarded it on to Cheshire with the words "shaky pollisie" underlined in red pencil and his own comment in the margin: "Not the only one."

Mrs. Chinnadorai wrote to say that she had heard of Cheshire's work and would like to help him by starting a Home for burnt-out leprosy patients somewhere in her part of India. Cheshire replied at once, approving of her plan and saying that he would help her to the best of his ability. He had very little money to offer her, but what he had was sent down to South India, where this tireless widow set about a search for a house in which to put some of the numerous lepers who are discharged from time to time from the great hospital at Vellore, where so much curative and research work is done in the field of leprosy. When the disease has burnt itself out, as Cheshire was coming to know, the sufferers who still retain the scars of the disease are not received back into their own villages and families, such is the prejudice against this illness among many people in Asia.

Mrs. Chinnadorai's search through much of South India lasted for nearly a year, but she never gave up hope. On several occasions she found suitable houses which appeared to be within her reach, but as soon as the neighbours discovered what she was planning to do pressure was brought to bear on the sellers, with the result that time and again she was frustrated at the very moment when she thought that success was within her grasp. At last her courage and perseverance were rewarded. She found a small one-storey bungalow with a courtyard in the centre. It was just off the main street of a village called Katpadi, five miles from the town of Vellore. Half the house was still occupied by tenants, and the courtyard was in an indescribable state. But it was a beginning. Cheshire's reason for encouraging Mrs. Chinnadorai to find a suitable property near Vellore was that he had met Dr. Ida Scudder, a doctor there, who had said to him: "Wouldn't it be lovely if you could have one of your Homes close to the hospital, so that we could work together?"

Cheshire realized only too well that he was a novice in this field, following in the steps of so many courageous and gifted people who had given their whole lives to tackling the terrible problem of leprosy. He came to realize that, whilst a great deal is being done for those who suffer from the disease, those who are incurable or burnt-out, in whom the infection is no longer alive but who must bear the scars of the disease for ever, are in the same position as most of the chronic sick throughout the world. He learned now that although the disease can be arrested, provided it is tackled early enough, nevertheless the effects remain, the claw hands and the facial disfigurement. Even more serious, there is a lack of sensation in the hands and feet, which means that the sufferers hurt themselves without knowing it, and, as the disease has already weakened their system, are more easily susceptible to injury than the rest of us. He thought he discerned, in these conditions, a small part of this enormous field in which he might, perhaps, be able to work by providing a sheltered home where burnt-out leprosy patients could be given loving care and protection. As in England, so in India he was probing behind the medical problem, which he knew only too well was not his sphere, to the social and human aspects—in the case of lepers, the fear and the ostracism of their neighbours, their need for a sheltered environment in which to live, and the opportunity of fulfilling their human hopes and aspirations.

Some time before this Phil Loneragan, the Australian girl, had come to India at Cheshire's request to help build up the necessary administration with which to underpin the work in this new part of the world, and had done much of the office work in Calcutta. Now she went to help Mrs. Chinnadorai start up the Home at Katpadi.

"My first feeling about Vishranti Illam," she told me later, "was one of complete funk. I just didn't know what to expect, except that I knew I didn't look forward to seeing a leper, much less being in close contact with one. But from the time Mrs. Chinnadorai's wide, beaming face met my slightly apprehensive gaze, a feeling of relief began to creep slowly over me; she looked so solid, sane and sensible—everything must be all right!

"As we walked from the bus to the Home, I remember her offering me her large black umbrella and my thanking her, but saying that in Australia we were quite used to the sun, and her kindness in opening it for us both when she saw I'd gone a delicate shade of puce after only covering half the distance. It was on this walk that she told me how she had become personally involved in the idea of this Home for the lepers, and we arrived at the Home just as she told me that the first had arrived only that morning. Back rushed my instinctive fear, but when I entered the room and met him, and he got up from his bed and stood on his poor crippled feet to welcome me, I just never had another feeling of fear or revulsion."

The house at Katpadi was filled up in no time with thirty burnt-out lepers who for some months were shunned by the neighbours, out of fear. But within a short space of time Mrs. Chinnadorai, through her energy and example, was able to build up a spirit of happiness and self-reliance in the new Home, for she insisted that the patients must each do something positive to occupy their time and to bring them in touch with the world outside. So they began to make toys from wooden boxes, which were not difficult to sell. They also made vases from the discarded tins of powdered milk which came to them through the Madras Government from the World Health Organization. They would cut out pieces from the sides of the tins, press the tins into the required shapes, all of them highly artistic, and then paint them in many different designs. Mrs. Chinnadorai watched over them carefully while they were at work, for, although the infection had left them, the parts of their bodies which had been affected had become insensitive to pain, so that it was possible for them inadvertently to damage themselves without knowing they had done so.

Mrs. Chinnadorai had dark hair which was turning white, and a charming smile. In her South Indian *saris* she looked maternal and very kind. The patients called her their "Mother," and in the evenings before they went to bed they would sing with her South Indian songs and hymns, their faces reflecting the happiness they had found with each other in this Home, which was trying so hard to replace the homes from which they had been barred by prejudice and ignorance. Cheshire has always said that this was the happiest of all the Homes. It was certainly the poorest so far as money was concerned, but when the inevitable happened, and the neighbours began to realize not only that these people were cured of their disease, and so were not infectious, but also that they seemed to be exceedingly happy in their active community life, they started to come round to the house. Before long they would come in the evenings to the singing, for Indians love music, and soon the children of the village had established many contacts with the cheerful lady whom they, too, began to call "Mother."

Michael, the schoolmaster with multiple sclerosis, a condition which is unusual in tropical latitudes, was able to find a place in the new Home at Covelong, twenty miles south of Madras on the sea front, in the house which was given to Cheshire at this time by the Bishop of Madras. Later he took up photography, and made a colour sound film of the Homes in India for a very small sum indeed. The film opened with some shots of the beach at Covelong and of the rollers and the surf of the Indian Ocean, which broke within fifty yards of this beautifully situated house.

The Home at Singapore which started at this time came about by an unforeseen but happy series of circumstances. Cheshire, during one of his visits to the monastery of Solesmes, had met a young French Count, François de Vallembreuse, who had offered to pay his own fare to whatever part of the world Cheshire should want to send him. He didn't guarantee to stay for a long time wherever he should be sent, but he wanted to find out if perhaps Cheshire's work was the sort of thing to which he might be called to devote his life.

Cheshire at this moment was ill in Bombay, where he was lying in St. Elizabeth's Nursing Home. Despite his decision at Midhurst that the chronic sick would be his life's work, at this particular moment he was unhappy about the part he was playing in the Foundation. The Homes in India were developing surprisingly well even without the Government subsidies which had been such a help to the work in England. Wherever he had been able to make a start—in Bombay, Calcutta, Delhi, Madras, Katpadi, Dehra Dun—helpers and committees had always been forthcoming to carry the heavy burden of founding and running the Homes out of local resources alone. So long as Cheshire had been personally involved in the work of getting the Homes started, and therefore in close contact with the patients, all had been well. But now, as the committees demonstrated their willingness and ability to stand on their own feet, he was being inexorably forced out of the Homes themselves into the role of an administrator. And for this he knew that he was not fitted, and never would be. With the appearance of François on the scene, a fit and young man of great initiative, talent and idealism, Cheshire began to wonder if Providence was not pointing the way to a partnership. Let François take over the task of founding and administering, while he retired from the centre of the stage and concentrated on the thing that seemed to him to be lacking—prayer. By this he did not mean just his own prayers, but a permanent framework of prayer built into the Foundation in some way that would not be contradicting its non-denominational character or false to his own beliefs as a Catholic.

Now he suddenly decided that he would put his idea to the test. He would take François to Singapore, where Pam Hickley, his cousin, and her husband lived, for the purpose of starting up a new Foundation. It was not just that the opportunity of starting in Singapore had been offered to him, but that Cheshire had for a long time been strongly attracted towards China, and was eager to take whatever appeared to be a step in its direction.

Two days after he and François arrived in Singapore there was large-scale rioting on the island and a total curfew was imposed. Pam Hickley, by virtue of her job as personal secretary to the chief of C.I.D., had a pass that enabled her to go where she wanted, and since she had by now made up her mind that a Home was badly needed in Singapore, she used it to the full. She arranged that either François or Leonard should see everyone whom she considered essential to the launching of the plan, and by the time the fortnight they were due to stay had almost run out they had the active support of the Ministry of Health, the Ministry of Social Welfare, the Press and radio, and a well-chosen representative committee. Even the Prison Commission had suggested work parties from the nearest jail. All that was needed was a house; but this, in view of the chronic state of overcrowding and the consequent inflated value of property, seemed all but an impossibility, at any rate if it had to be acquired for nothing.

Then one day, quite by chance, Cheshire and François came across the remains of an old Army gun-site near the beautiful Changi Beach, on the eastern end of the island. It was ruined and roofless; and the Treasury in Whitehall (for it still belonged to the Army) showed no vestige of sympathy or interest in Cheshire's plan, and demanded either a rental of £600 a year or a purchase price of five figures plus. Before this chilly piece of information came through from Whitehall, the committee had held its first meeting and agreed to start a Home out of the ruins. It was a brave decision, for not only was the political situation very uncertain, with Independence approaching and the danger of further rioting, but François did not feel that he could commit himself to more than part-time and intermittent help—which, in the years since, he has given most generously. Cheshire, on the other hand, though finally convinced that it was useless looking for someone to whom he could delegate his own role, made it clear that he could only return at very infrequent intervals, perhaps not even once a year. Yet the committee, led by his cousin Pam, were not to be put off.

At this stage it was Phil Loneragan who stepped into the breach, travelling to Singapore to run the spacious office that had unexpectedly been given in the very heart of the city, and to pass on to the committee the experience gained in starting Homes in England and India. Out of the blue, the new Malayan Government bought the site from the Treasury and gave it to the committee on an indefinite lease for a token one dollar annual rent. This proved the signal for a flood of voluntary help, led by the almost non-stop work parties from the R.A.F. and including prisoners from Changi Jail as well as Rotary, Toc H and other organizations, which perhaps exceeded even that at Staunton Harold. Within barely six months a Home with fourteen beds had been built without a single farthing being spent on labour or any form of professional service, an example that was to be followed on an even larger scale eighteen months later—this time with the Army in the lead—at Johore Bahru in the Federation of Malaya.

It was the Singapore committee which was responsible for discovering the emblem that has been adopted by many of the Homes in different parts of the world, the red feather. Red in many parts of Asia is regarded as the colour which is symbolical of joy and happiness, so in Singapore they decided to call one of the balls, which they had organized to raise funds for the Home at Changi, the Red Feather Ball.

Although in some ways the story of the Singapore Home is one of the most successful so far recorded, it was not without many difficulties. Phil did not like Singapore, but she stayed as long as she could. When at last she left to return to England, a crisis blew up in the Home, caused by a clash of personalities among some of the voluntary workers. Most of the Homes have in fact experienced a similar situation at some stage of their development, but in this case the clash was so violent and irreconcilable that the committee feared that everything would disintegrate and be lost.

Pam cabled Leonard in India, imploring him to come and help, saying that she would never dream of making such a request were it not that it was the only means of saving the Home. Had it been two years previously, he would have dropped everything and gone immediately, but he was beginning to learn that in a crisis, particularly if it is one of human relations, the better course is not always to rush hurriedly in. And he had engagements in India which he was reluctant to break.

On balance he decided that it would be wrong to go. If the Home were to founder just because he couldn't get there himself, then its future couldn't be very secure; sooner or later it would founder for some reason which might be beyond his control. From all points of view it was better that it should face the issue here and now and either win or lose. It is to the Home's lasting credit that, thanks in good measure to an entirely new and unexpected personality who turned up on the scene, it not only solved all its difficulties but has gone from strength to strength ever since, with no support or assistance of any kind from outside the island. Today it has been entrusted with the task of acting as the focal point for South-East Asia. And its little red feathers are pinned to many a dress and *sarong* and *sari* and blouse in Europe and Asia, India and Africa.

CHAPTER EIGHT

"THE TRUST"

DURING THE WINTER of 1955-6 it did seem for a while in England as if the doubters might have been right and that no more Homes would start. The Trustees were feeling their way, and were certainly in no hurry to accept into the fold any new Home about whose finances and stability they were at all doubtful. There had been one almighty row down at St. Teresa's, and there were signs that all was not well at St. Cecilia's. A Christmas appeal in *The Times* brought in £9 2*s*. Would the whole thing fizzle out while its founder was absent and very silent somewhere among the jungles and sprawling cities of India?

Then, in April, a curious and significant thing happened: a Yorkshire engineer formed a committee in Halifax, and a second group of people got together in York. Both these groups started collecting money and organizing support for the Cheshire Homes without showing any sign of having heard of the Trustees in London, and quite independently of one another. It was, in fact, somewhat typical of the North of England. The significance of these ventures was their spontaneity, and the fact that they were made in a distant part of England far from the pioneer Homes and the protection and patronage of the Trustees. They also happened to concide with my own arrival in England.

A few weeks earlier, under the mango trees at Bethlehem House, Cheshire, who was then on his second visit to India, had asked me if I would work for him in England. I had said I would, and when I got back to

London in the spring of 1956 I called at the home in Smith Square of Sir Archibald Jamieson, the financier who had helped St. Cecilia's, and who was now the Honorary Treasurer of the Cheshire Foundation Homes for the Sick. Reluctantly, he had come to the conclusion that he must relinquish that position, and the suggestion was that I should take it on. I was relieved to discover that I had met Sir Archibald ten years before, when he had been Chairman of Vickers Armstrong, of which company my old firm had been the agents in India. We took a taxi to the Law Courts, where I was to be introduced to Sir Alfred Denning, and as we bowled along the Embankment he told me that it was in Sir Alfred's rooms that the infrequent meetings of the Trust took place. This very tall man, whose legs could scarcely squeeze into the taxi, was friendly and relaxed. He seemed to think it was a good thing that a newcomer from abroad—and one in his early forties—should be coming to join them.

"We need some younger blood," he commented. "Apart from Leonard himself we're all a bit ancient, and likely to fall off our perches at any minute."

He had then described each Trustee in turn, humorously and with surprising frankness; most of them were well-known in their different spheres of activity.

When we reached the Law Courts and I was introduced to Sir Alfred Denning I sensed at once that I was on inspection, although they couldn't have been nicer about it. In India there are so many religions that one soon stops thinking about this particular difference between one's colleagues in so far as everyday life is concerned. The committees and boards in the midst of which I had been living and working for so many years had all had their customary representatives of the different communities and of the Hindus of castes and sub-castes. So it came as rather a shock, in the matter-of-fact surroundings of Sir Alfred's book-lined room looking out on to Carey Street, to be asked what my religion was. The Judge could only have been an Anglican, and I had no idea about Sir Archibald; later, I learned that he was a Roman Catholic. When I said a shade emphatically that I belonged to the Church of England, I sensed that the Judge was relieved, although this feeling may well have been hindsight.

As Sir Archibald and I drove back to his Queen Anne house in Westminster he said: "There's not much to hand over, apart from some money a friend and I have put in, which we would rather like to be used at St. Cecilia's. It's the responsibility for looking after it and for getting in some more which rather daunts me, I'm afraid, especially as I shall be travelling a lot out of England."

In his panelled drawing-room he thanked me for taking on this job, and spoke with feeling about Leonard Cheshire.

"He's an extraordinary young man. I'm many years older than he is; yet his generation did so much in the war that when it was over I felt I had to see his peacetime efforts get off to a start of some kind. He needs some solid people to keep him on the rails, but they mustn't be too old and too solid or they will pull against him. That's why I'm delighted you're going in. Good luck."

Not long afterwards I learnt that he had lost a son in the war who had been awarded a posthumous V.C.

For a little over twelve months, while I was looking for a new career in England, I had a seat in the London office of my old firm in India, so there was time to spare in between job-hunting and the not very onerous duties of the office to put in some work, if it should be required, for the Cheshire Trustees.

At the first meeting I attended, held while Cheshire was still in India, I could sense that the half-dozen Trustees, most of whom have appeared already in this story, had no very firm idea of where they were going, and were indeed not a little fearful of the implications, particularly on the financial side, of further development. The keynote seemed to be a caution which expressed itself in an unwillingness to take on new Homes unless they had proved themselves to be sound as regards both administration and money; in fact, when the initiative of the people of York and Halifax was reported at this meeting it was decided they must be told that the Trust could not consider accepting their Homes until they had been going for at least a year. Looking back, I can see now how important these happenings were, leading inevitably to the development of these and other Homes in the north of England as sturdy, independent units which, as they grew from strength to strength, were held rather at arm's length from the Trust, which remained to some extent a southern body.

"And then there's this worrying business of Wardour Castle," Sir Alfred Denning said after we had disposed of the news from the North.

"Here is a letter from the warden saying that we must spend several hundred pounds at once on the ceilings of the main rooms, where he has put the patients, simply to keep the plaster from falling down on to their heads. He hints that long-term repairs may run into thousands. I wonder what we ought to do about it, because he doesn't seem to be getting a great deal of help or advice from his committee. I wonder if someone could possibly go down there to see what it's all about."

As I had just joined up and seemed to have fewer commitments than the others, and also, I suppose, because I was now in charge of the finances, I agreed to drive down to Wiltshire to see what it was all about. And it was in this way that I visited my first Cheshire Home in England. I met the committee, and was quite prepared to accept their straightforward explanations for the lack of local support, which they attributed, understandably, to the isolation of the Castle and the absence of any industrial towns in the neighbourhood. There was no mention of the ex-gaolbirds who were Cheshire's real reason for wanting to get Wardour Castle going, probably because the committee had as little inkling of Cheshire's intentions in this matter as the Trustees; although the intermittent and disturbing appearance in their midst of these former prisoners must have unnerved them and contributed to the general uncertainty and lack of confidence.

I came back to London with some pretty devastating figures supplied by the warden and his architect, and at the next meeting of the Trustees brought the former into the discussion. He laid before Sir Alfred and the others a stark picture which showed that at least sixty thousand pounds would be needed to make the house safe to live in, and another considerable amount to furnish and shape the interior as a nursing-home. The Historic Buildings Council had indicated that they would consider meeting quite a proportion of the costs of the architectural reconstruction, but that would still leave a hefty responsibility for conversion and the recurring expenditure of running the Home, both of which were clearly beyond our powers and those of the local committee. And so, in Cheshire's absence, the Trustees decided to close down Wardour Castle, the legacy of a previous period and an experiment of which they almost certainly would not have approved if they had appreciated what it was all about. If Cheshire had been in England, I doubt if he would have let us do it, although where the money and the support would have come from I can't imagine. He has in fact admitted that both his methods and his timing on this one were wrong, so that we can assume once more that Providence wished it to happen in this way, and while he was abroad.

At this same meeting the Trustees felt that one of them really ought to go up North to visit the two new Homes, Alne Hall and White Windows, and to meet their committees. As the new recruit I seemed to be the obvious person to go, and although at the time I felt quite inexperienced and was still under the impression that everyone in England knew what he was doing, and was doing it in a highly professional way—part of the inferiority complex most exiles have about the way things are run at home, until they come to live there and learn the truth—I am glad I went right at the beginning of the northern Homes' existence, and of my own connection with the movement.

Alne Hall is a pleasant house in the country fourteen miles north of York. When I got there in the middle of summer the countryside was looking its best, but the garden round the house was neglected and there was clearly much work to be done. The group of people who had started the Home, and who are much the same today, were getting on quietly with the job of bringing in patients, organizing support, and making the necessary alterations to the house in such a determined and independent way that it was quite clear the venture would succeed and that they would need no help from the Trustees in far-off London. I did not appreciate at the time that this attitude of the people of Yorkshire was proof that Cheshire had found the right formula for the solution of this particular problem in the British Isles, and that from now on it would be a question of applying the formula in the correct numbers and the correct places.

At Alne Hall I met one of the band of women who would gradually become the spearhead of his mission overseas. Anne Thomas, the matron, was a young woman who seemed, even to my inexperienced eyes, to be devoted to this rather unusual kind of work. I told her a little of the background of the only Home I knew about personally, the three asbestos cement huts in the jungles of Salsette Island outside Bombay, and perhaps this may have lit a spark in her imagination, for three years later

Le Court—old and new

Le Court—dining-room

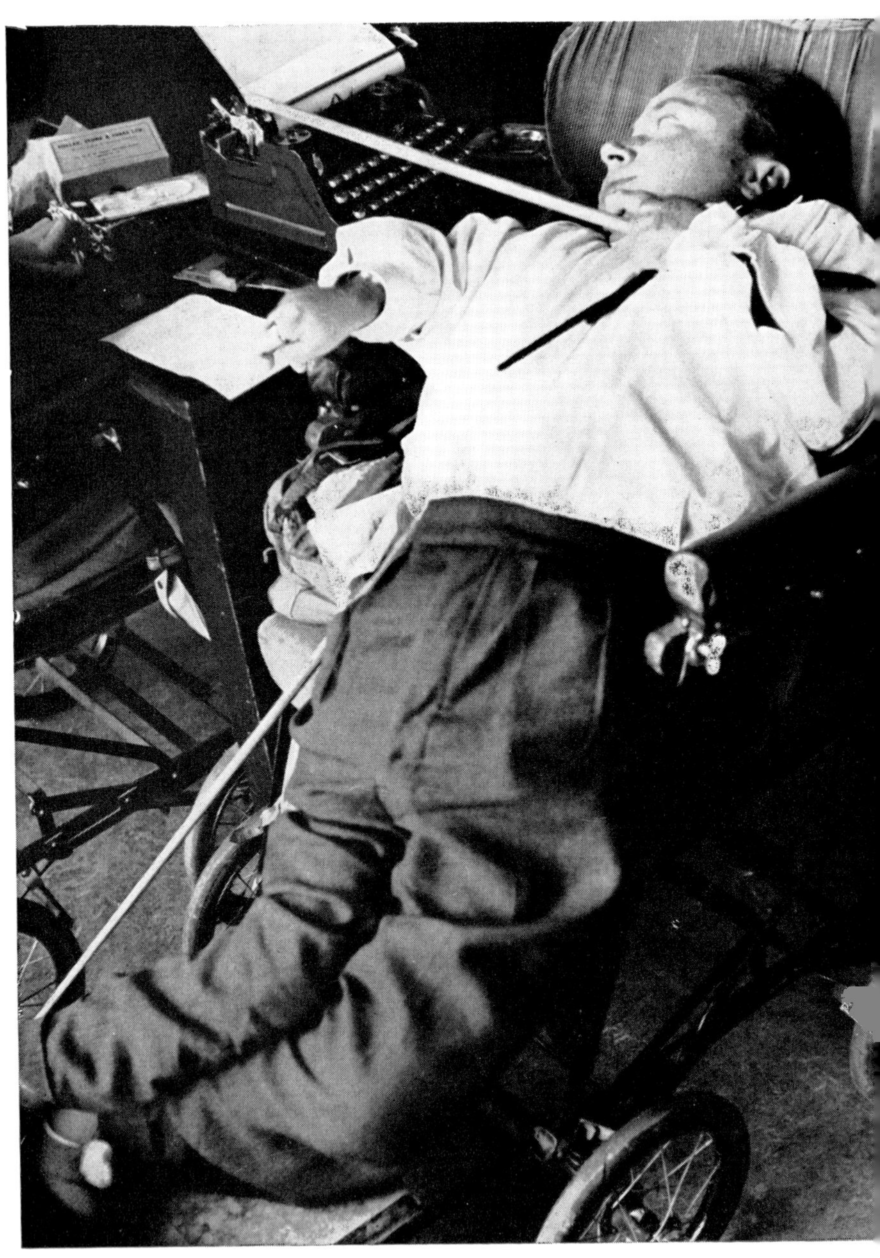

Lenny at St. Teresa's working his typewriter with a special wooden prong

The leper colony at Raphael. Ava Dhar is in a white sari in the foreground

The children's home at Raphael—old

The children's home at Raphael—new

View across the dried-up riverbed of the Rispana. The leper colony can be seen among the trees on the far bank

Raphael: leper children learning to write. They spread sand over a board and use a stick

Two patients at the Delhi Home. The boy on the right, who has tuberculosis of the spine, is paralysed from the waist down

The children in the Oluwole Home; Margot Mason is standing in

she went abroad to Jordan, where she built up a children's Home on foundations laid by Margot Mason. She is still carrying on the work there.

Then I went to Halifax in the West Riding, where the engineer had succeeded in buying a fine house complete with beds, crockery and linen from a textile company which had used it previously as a hostel for women weavers from the Continent. He and his friends had bought it at a remarkably low price, since the textile firm had wished to make their own contribution to the project. Here, too, I met the solid, enthusiastic and energetic committee members who were beginning to set the pattern which was to become characteristic of the whole country, and later of Wales and Scotland. This pattern now became more and more a local one, with the initiative being taken in a county, a town or a district. The Trust in London was a convenient legal repository for the properties as they were acquired, since nominal ownership of the increasing number of houses was assigned to the Trust, with whom the deeds were lodged. Everything else—administration, fund-raising, admission of patients—was the sole responsibility of the Home itself. As one would expect, and as it became clear to me on this visit to the first two Homes in the North of England, the Trustees would not be looked to for help or advice or admonition. The local committees just got on with the job, and therein lay their source of strength as the movement gained its second wind. Both Alne Hall and White Windows already had a few patients during this summer of 1956, and were only waiting for the installation of their lifts, for which they had already raised the funds, before taking in the maximum number of thirty patients in each case.

I came back to London with the conviction that Cheshire's presence was certainly not necessary for starting new Homes, as it had evidently been in the beginning and as it certainly was in India. I had also seen with my own eyes that many people in widely differing walks of life wanted something to which they could devote their energies now that the State had taken over the hospitals.

Back in London the Trustees were still feeling their way, the fear of financial collapse ever present in their minds. This fear was justified, but it did have the result of holding at arm's length these new groups of people who had to use Cheshire's name in order to get their projects moving, yet who were not accepted into the family at the moment of their first enthusiasm. This widening gap might have resulted in the movement disintegrating into unrelated pockets of activity all over the country, but happily this did not happen, for early in the following year, by an extraordinary chance, an unexpected financial strength was injected into the Trust in a manner so strange that I have never really understood quite how or why it happened.

Phil had gone back to Australia, and Margot had now moved into a larger room in the same mews cottage, a bed-sitting-room on the first floor. This had become her home in London, and also the office, which was moved upstairs from the passage below. Then the landlords told us that they had received notice to quit; a great new hotel was to be built on the site, and the mews was to be pulled down. Just as we were taking in this news and wondering where on earth we should go, a landowner in Lincolnshire who had been an air commodore in Bomber Command in the war wrote to Sir Alfred Denning with an interesting and unusual offer. He said that he and his family wished to give the Foundation a house in Lincolnshire in memory of their parents. They wanted to make the gift in such a way as to give the maximum benefit to Cheshire's work, to which end he proposed that they should either present it outright to the Trust, or, if we should have the money available, they would sell the house and its gardens to us for seven thousand pounds and make a covenant in favour of the Trust of one thousand pounds a year for seven years, thereby increasing their gift by the amount of income tax which one could claim on each annual contribution. The house, we soon discovered, was worth at least twelve thousand pounds, and was ideal for transformation into a Cheshire Home, so that we should be the gainers by something like five thousand pounds over the period, if we could find the money with which to make the initial purchase.

We were in Sir Alfred's rooms in the Law Courts.

"We haven't got anything like that sum, have we?" Sir Alfred looked at me enquiringly, and I had to reply that we had already eaten into the generous gifts of the previous Treasurer and his friend which had been earmarked for St. Cecilia's.

"I'm afraid there's nothing like the sum needed in our account, and we simply have to hang on to the regular flow of donations which come in from all over the country in smallish amounts in order to keep the office and organization going," I replied.

These donations, from churches, schools, Rotary Clubs and groups in factories up and down the country, came to about three hundred pounds a month, which was a great deal, but not in the class of money we now required.

"And there's another thing, Sir Alfred," I said at this meeting. "You know we're being kicked out of Pitts Head Mews. Well, we've just heard of an ideal place for the office and where Margot could live. It's a small maisonette in a mews not a hundred yards from our present office, and we can get a ninety-nine-year lease with a tiny ground tent. The snag about this property, which is brand new, is that the price of the lease is eight thousand pounds. But spread over ninety-nine years, and including the ground rent, the cost would be less than a hundred pounds a year."

It was a distressing situation, both on account of the fine gesture of the ex-air commodore and his family, and because of the extraordinary chance of having almost within our grasp a home and an office for Margot Mason within a stone's throw of the old one. But our account could be reckoned in hundreds where we required thousands.

Sir Alfred thought for a minute or two, and then said: "You're a business-man. What about seeing the bank? Do you think they would help?"

It seemed a forlorn hope. I had borrowed money many a time in my business career, but always for well-founded industrial companies which could supply ample security and to which banks were anxious to make loans. Nevertheless, the more we discussed the problem the clearer it became that this was the only thing to do, for another consideration had come into my mind. Sir Alfred Denning had recently been made a peer, and would in future sit on the Judicial Committee of the House of Lords. We should no longer be able to have our meetings in his rooms in the Law Courts. The situation was rather desperate.

The next morning I called on the manager of the branch of the Westminister Bank in Bishopsgate where the Trust's account was kept. I was shown straight into his office. He had received many odd visitors in that room, and he showed admirable politeness in welcoming what he must have known could not be a profitable account. Then we got talking, for he had heard of Cheshire and was interested in his doings.

"Where is he at the moment?"

I replied that he would soon be returning to England from his second winter in India.

"Would it be possible to meet him, I wonder? I have an idea that one or two of our general managers would like to have a talk with him."

I had explained in a few words and with much

trepidation the position in which we found ourselves, with two excellent opportunities before us, one of which would give us a beautiful Home for thirty patients in Lincolnshire and would at the same time present us with what amounted to an additional five thousand pounds in cash with which the work could be still further extended: and the other an ideal office and home for our secretary in the heart of London, which would cost us no more, over a century, than a hundred pounds a year. I hardly dared mention the figure of fifteen thousand pounds which we should have to have in our hands in order to take advantage of these offers.

A few days later Cheshire flew back from India, and almost simultaneously there was an invitation from the Westminster Bank for both of us to have lunch with the general managers in Lothbury, the head office in the City. It was a pleasant lunch with a group of pleasant men. Cheshire talked about India most of the time. He never mentioned money. A week later the manager of the Bishopsgate Branch, whose name was John Handscomb, asked me round to his office.

He spoke in the same friendly and almost casual tones as during our first interview.

"I have heard from my head office. They have agreed to this branch giving your Trust an overdraft up to a limit of eighteen thousand five hundred pounds at a special rate of interest."

"But what about security?" I asked.

"Well, I expect there are some title deeds to the various properties, aren't there? We shouldn't want them all, but perhaps a few of them might be deposited here; nothing formal."

I didn't believe it for a few minutes—in fact, it was only the calmness of his voice which finally persuaded me that I had heard correctly. Then I asked him if I could telephone Lord Denning. Not long afterwards John Handscomb visited one of the Homes, and soon after that he relieved me of the responsibilities of being Honorary Treasurer, for I had now started on my second career, which was to involve much travelling outside England and a very full day's work when I was in the country. We bought Hovenden House in Lincolnshire and Number Seven, Market Mews, in Mayfair.

This astonishing and unexpected financial backing did a great deal more than enable us to buy the lease of Market Mews and a beautiful house in the country; it gave just that degree of confidence to the Trustees which we seemed to need at this time, so that we were able to move more rapidly and surely towards a position of influence and later of control over policy which the spreading movement needed, if it was to retain any cohesion and if the ground was to be consolidated behind its wayward and incalculable founder.

This growing confidence was invaluable in tackling two rather unpleasant tasks which were handed to me by Lord Denning during this summer of 1957—in fact, I seemed to be the dog's-body of the Trust at this time. On the first occasion I was thrown in at the deep end with a vengeance, for the position at St. Cecilia's had become critical. The managing committee of the Home was seriously divided into two distinct groups of people, who took opposing views on almost every point of policy and administration. The root of the problem, as I saw it, was the fact that the chairman of the committee was a doctor. Cheshire felt strongly that a doctor was not the right person to hold such a position, and he supported the decision of Lord Denning and the Trustees that the chairman should be asked to resign and that Bob Worthington, the founder of the Home, should take his place. It is not surprising that such drastic action created antagonism among many good friends of the Home in Bromley, resignations from the committee, and a feeling that the Trustees were acting from prejudice. It was an unpleasant business, but the new chairman soon rallied a united committee to a fresh advance, which included the construction of a modern wing to accommodate all the patients of the existing Home and a dozen more. This was the first occasion when the Trustees in London exerted their authority by reconstituting the management committee of a Home; not long afterwards they followed it up by another exercise of authority in more dramatic circumstances which involved my second intervention as the representative of the central body.

Winter had come, my first in England for many years, and I found it very hard. On a bitter night Margot Mason and I went down by train to Ampthill Park House, for the roads were so covered by ice that we could not take the car. We had been asked by Lord Denning to attend a meeting of the management committee of this Home, for, despite its inspiring start under Paul Latham, and the fact that Cheshire had spent a lot of time there himself in the early days during the previous winter, it had not been as successful as some of the other Homes. Cheshire's original idea that this particular Home should be set aside especially for T.B. cases had not come off, since there were happily fewer and fewer sufferers from this disease requiring accommodation. Consequently, a number of the conventional type of Cheshire patients had been brought into Ampthill, but there had not been anything like enough money to install a lift—you need at least two thousand five hundred pounds to put in an invalid-type lift in the sort of house that normally comes our way—with the result that the patients could only be placed in the spacious ground floor rooms. This meant that it was difficult to segregate the sexes. So there were no women among the twenty patients at Ampthill, and the atmosphere, even to an outsider like myself, did not seem to have the lightness and the spontaneity of the other Homes.

As has happened from time to time, the unhappiness which seemed clear enough to us on the outside was not as evident to some of the local committee. There was a deadlock with the Trustees in London, who had hoped that the committee would put their house in order without our intervention. Since this had not happened, it had become clear that the Trustees must take action.

There can be few things more distasteful than upsetting the domestic affairs of good people who are working for the same end as oneself, and in their spare time. But it seemed to all of us that this was unavoidable if another Home was not to go on the rocks. Margot Mason and I spent a cold, unhappy evening at Ampthill, at the end of which there was a new chairman and a new committee, but no warden and no matron to look after the Home and the twenty disabled patients. I got back to London very late, while she stayed behind and took over the rambling house with all its problems and the unhappy atmosphere which we had inevitably created. I felt angry in the empty carriage of the midnight train at the false position in which we had been placed and at the hurtful words that had been said, yet I knew how I should feel if the position had been reversed and some forceful stranger from London had come down out of the night to criticize my voluntary work and turn it upside down.

Le Court came to the rescue and arranged for an Irish girl, Mia, who was their efficient secretary, to come over the next day in order to keep Margot Mason company. These two, with their experience and humour, backed up the new chairman and his new committee, who rose to the occasion and surmounted the crisis. The patients, who knew that something was seriously wrong, also helped in a way that is difficult to describe, for they somehow gave to the forces that were fighting so hard to save their community the encouragement of their own unity and newly discovered happiness.

I went down several times in the following weeks, and found myself wondering how this extraordinary situation could possibly continue, for there was very little money and so little experience among the small group of people on the committee. There were no rich or titled people, no men of particular influence in the county. Could it possibly last? The fact that it did, and that in a matter of weeks Margot and Mia could return to their jobs, is a tribute to the committee and to the committee system; it is also a tribute to the growing confidence and character of the Trust, which had not flinched at grasping two uncomfortable nettles, and in so doing had saved at least one Cheshire home from the unhappiness and ignominy of closure.

CHAPTER NINE

WEST AFRICA

DURING THE NEXT two or three years I had the opportunity of visiting, and in some cases helping to bring into being, many of the new Homes which were starting up in other countries. For the second career on which I had embarked early in 1958 involved a good deal of travelling, and I was able to combine my professional work and work for the Cheshire Homes. I had joined a development bank in the City which was charged with the specific task of providing long-term finance for new industries in the emerging countries of the Commonwealth. I happened to join it at a moment when it had been asked by the Government of Nigeria to organize and establish a development bank in that country, for Nigeria was due for political independence in 1960. So through most of 1958 I found myself flying to and fro between London and Lagos.

During these visits—not only to Lagos, but also to Ibadan and Kano and Enugu—I met many people of many races. In the course of these contacts, and the many conversations which grew from them, there was inevitably talk of the Cheshire Homes. In Ibadan, the large and almost completely African town which lies a hundred and twenty miles due north of Lagos and is the capital of the go-ahead Western Region, I called at the impressive new University College Hospital, which had been built shortly before with funds provided by the British Government and had been designed by the same architect as Le Court. Almost the first doctor I met was an Irishman who was in charge of the chest clinic. After he had taken me round the out-patients' department, which seemed to be full to overflowing with mothers and their babies, most of whom were suffering from beriberi, he took me into his office for a cold drink, for it was hot and sticky. I told him a little of Cheshire and what he was trying to do, and there was an instant reaction. The need was great in Nigeria, he said, particularly among the children. I already knew, from an Englishwoman to whom I had talked in Lagos, that there were many crippled children who, because they were deformed, were kept by their parents at the back of the village hut in obscurity and darkness so that the family's disgrace should not become a matter for scorn. Perhaps it was the never-ending flow of cases, especially of children, perhaps it was his Irish temperament which determined his attitude; whatever it was, he said he would do his utmost to get a Home going in Ibadan as soon as he came back from leave, for he was off in a week's time. But how should he set about it? We arranged to meet in Market Mews while he was on his way through London to Dublin. With any luck, Cheshire might be back from India, and they could meet.

The Irish doctor duly met Cheshire in Market Mews. Then he went off to Dublin for his leave. On my next trip to Lagos a few weeks later, I took with me a copy of the B.B.C. film of Le Court and also a message from Cheshire specially recorded on tape. The interest had not taken long to grow, particularly in Ibadan. In the following spring, March, 1959, Margot Mason made the first of a series of journeys which were to take place regularly from now on, in the period before the annual spring conference in London.

She had experienced many hardships in India, so I was not worried about that side of it, but from what I had seen of Africa, during my half-dozen fleeting visits to Nigeria, there might be more frustrations than in India. And she would be on her own.

I was able to meet her at Ikeja airport. I got there just as the sun was rising. As I walked through the main entrance I noticed an elderly-looking European woman sitting by herself with a little bundle of luggage beside her. She looked very patient and very tired. It was unusual to see a European woman of her age in West Africa; alone and waiting outside the airport entrance, it was even more unusual. I passed through to the information desk. There were a lot of people waiting to meet the London plane, and when the aircraft touched down they all pressed forward to meet the passengers they knew. Margot Mason came down the gangway last. I thought I should be the only one left of the crowd of visitors, and was surprised to find myself beaten through the little gate by two large Roman Catholic fathers, an officer in the Nigerian Police Force, two British soldiers and the elderly Englishwoman. There were more people to meet Margot than anyone else on the plane.

The fathers had come from the Archbishop, an eighty-year-old Irish prelate who had spent nearly sixty years in Nigeria. The policeman was a friend of Lady Denning. I never discovered how the soldiers fitted in. And the elderly Englishwoman, whose name was Flora Tassell, had come the afternoon before from Ghana, where she had been working for many years at a mission station in the bush. She had written to Cheshire saying that she had heard he was coming to Nigeria, and had asked if she could work for him. Margot Mason had replied suggesting that she should come to Lagos as soon as a plan had been formulated. And here she was, having spent the night on a bench at Ikeja airport, in case she might miss the Group Captain's secretary in the morning. She had no money.

Our friends in Lagos put her up until Margot was ready two days later to move on to Ibadan, for it had not taken her long to decide that this was where the first Nigerian Home must be. The doctor was waiting for her, and together they found an empty house. Finding the owner was more difficult, and it took the best part of a fortnight to get him to agree to let it for a year at a figure that looked possible from the fund-raising point of view.

Margot had been to Government House, and been told there that the Red Cross was responsible for the sort of thing she wanted to do. And, anyway, it couldn't be done. From Government House she went to the house of Chief Awolowo, Chief Minister of the Western Region. When he understood what she was planning to do, he promised his support. The idea of an Englishwoman coming on her own to Nigeria to start a home for crippled African children without making demands on public funds and with no publicity seemed to him something worth supporting. He had been presented a few days before by some keen members of his party, the Action Group, with a cow.

"Would you like my cow for your home?"

She was delighted. The Chief Minister had no objection to the cow being sold, and the first donation to the Oluyole Cheshire Home in Ibadan, the first in Africa, came appropriately from the Chief Minister of the region in which it started.

The house they had found needed attention, as it had been empty for a year. Before that it had been neglected, and the drains were blocked up. The Irish doctor arranged for a contractor to clear them. Then he put a notice in the paper saying how grateful the committee had been that the contractor had done such noble work for the new Cheshire Home. As soon as the drains were unblocked, Flora Tassell moved in with three disabled children. Before she left, Margot Mason formed a committee, of which half the members were European and half African.

In this way the Cheshire movement went into West

Africa. It was especially interesting to me to see how smoothly and naturally it took root; and Africans seemed to take to the idea as readily as the expatriate Europeans, though, as elsewhere, there were a few of the latter who did much of the preliminary work. But it was the swift comprehension of the idea by Africans, and of the rightness of Cheshire's technique, which surprised me, as it had done in India. Not only had Margot Mason, with the help of many Africans and British, and particularly of the Irish doctor, started a Cheshire Home in Nigeria, but she had also got together the nucleus of a Nigerian Foundation under the Chairmanship of the Chief Justice, Sir Adetokumbo Ademola.

I had always been a believer in the Commonwealth, and had been happy when India decided to stay within it after she had gained her independence. In my new job with a Commonwealth development bank I had become even more enthusiastic; and since the seed sown by Cheshire seemed to germinate so rapidly in Commonwealth soil I tended to think that Cheshire's overseas work should concentrate on Commonwealth countries. But as time passed and the work spread, particularly in Sierra Leone, where I was going more frequently now than to Nigeria, it became clear that Cheshire had no intention of confining his overseas work to Commonwealth countries, either because it was easier or for any other reason. It would have been comparatively simple to have gone into Kenya, from where there had been several invitations; and I expect he will go there in time. His plans for the eastern side of Africa were to reveal themselves a year or two later, and they were directed at Ethiopia.

It always surprised me, as I travelled in different parts of the world, that so many people knew of Cheshire and his work. From a casual talk over a drink or at a dinner party, it often seemed that people wanted to know more; so the next time I went that way I would take a copy of a

B.B.C. film, or perhaps a tape-recorded message from Cheshire himself which would be put over the local radio network. And soon they would say that not only was there a need for a Home in their country, but they were sure they could get one going if only two things could be arranged—if someone from the Cheshire organization could show them how it was done, and if that person could perhaps bring some money.

When I tried to tell them that we would certainly send someone out as soon as it could be arranged, but that there could be very little in the way of money, their faces would fall. And when I told them that Cheshire never looked for patients, never called for helpers and never appealed for funds they were unbelieving. It was impossible to be rude by telling them they were wrong, especially as these people were just the ones who would soon be doing the very things they had said at the beginning were impossible.

An illustration of the Cheshire idea germinating and flourishing in an unlikely place is the story of Sierra Leone, the small country on the west coast of Africa which had begun its life early in the nineteenth century when Freetown was created by the British Government, in the days of Wilberforce, as a home for the slaves who had been intercepted by the Royal Navy on their way from Nigeria to the Caribbean.

Compared with Nigeria, Sierra Leone is small and poor, with one-twentieth of the people and considerably less economic wealth. But the people are proud and well educated—both the Creoles of the old colony on the island and the inhabitants of the interior, the Protectorate, as it used to be known. Fourah Bay College, perched on the cliffs of the mountain above Freetown, has given scholars and teachers to Nigeria, Ghana and the Gambia for well over a century. It has strong feelings of sympathy and friendship for the more powerful and wealthy Nigeria. It was natural, therefore, when I went there from Nigeria in 1960 for the third time, that I should speak to several people about the children's Home which the Nigerians had established in Ibadan. There seemed to be an immediate response, and somehow they seemed to cotton on at once to the idea of doing the same thing themselves.

Sitting with the Governor and his wife one evening under their pongam tree on the lovely terrace of Government House, we began to talk about it all. The next evening my hostess and I discussed it in greater detail and at greater length.

"It sounds to me," she said, "just the sort of thing we could all do well here. The Red Cross does a lot, but it's inevitably a bit official and connected, I suppose, in most people's minds with the British. Well, we shall be leaving soon, and I think the Cheshire idea would have a strong appeal both in Sierra Leone and in Freetown, for it would be something which might develop naturally along with independence, especially with all the different communities joining in."

So in February, 1961, the year of Sierra Leone's independence, Margot Mason set forth on a journey which was to be different in character from any she had undertaken before. In the course of it she was to set up two new Homes. Before she arrived in Freetown early in March she went to Tangier, for the ninety-year-old aunt of a friend in England had asked her to investigate the possibilities of a Cheshire Home.

She found great difficulties, and was met with outraged protests from the international community. But she sowed the seed so effectively that they now have one of the happiest children's Homes of the many all around the world. Then she went on to Sierra Leone, with only ten days to get something going there.

The justification for telling in some detail the story of the Sir Milton Cheshire Home at Bo is that it illustrates one of Cheshire's most firmly held beliefs—that just as it does not need powerful or wealthy people to relieve suffering, so it can prove to be as easy to build a Home and a family in a small territory unendowed with natural wealth and a large population as in rich and populous countries. Perhaps, even, it is easier.

She arrived only a few weeks before independence. Freetown was in a turmoil preparing for the great day in April, and for the week of celebrations in which many notables from foreign countries were to take part. People could think and talk of nothing else. Into this situation Margot Mason stepped with lightness and humour.

Before the first day was out she had gathered the nucleus of a Trust and had seen several properties, none of which seemed suitable. The next day, a Saturday, she was flown to Bo, a provincial town and an administrative headquarters a hundred and thirty miles inland from Freetown.

She found several people who agreed to form a committee, and she saw a house. It was rather tumbledown, but seemed quite a possibility. Then they flew back to Freetown. Before leaving Bo, she was told that the house belonged to the Prime Minister, Sir Milton Margai.

The next night the Governor and his wife had invited people from all the communities of the capital to Government House to see the film. It was *The Pathfinder*, made by the B.B.C. for television, and shown in England in Christmas week of 1959. All the Ministers had accepted invitations, including Sir Milton Margai.

Sir Milton is not communicative by nature; he has shrewdness and a sense of humour. When she was introduced to him before the film she mentioned that she had seen his house at Bo. The taciturn Prime Minister said nothing, and she found the going difficult. She assumed that his mind was on the arrangements for independence.

Then they went inside, the lights were put out and she

found herself sitting next to Sir Milton. Before long she heard him making exclamations of delight, particularly when any of the patients in the Cheshire Homes came on the screen.

Near the end of the first reel the producer takes viewers to the Home for mentally handicapped children at Dorchester. He chose a beautiful summer's day for shooting his pictures, and the children were out in the garden playing in a rubber paddling-pool. One of the girls who look after them explains at this point in the commentary that nobody has discovered how these dreadful circumstances arise, and what tragic situations these children can unwittingly create for their parents and families.

Suddenly in the darkness she sensed the Prime Minister leaning towards her. He was saying something to her. The commentary didn't make it easy for her to hear what he was saying. He had to repeat himself:

"You can have my house."

She could scarcely believe her ears. But it was true. In the letter she wrote describing this incident she said:

"It was thrilling. He was so kind afterwards, and said: 'Take it and use it. I don't want any money for it.' So—we need May Cutler."

Two days later she flew up to Bo again, and this time the Governor's wife went with her. She said she would start in herself to clean up the house.

It had once been a nursing home, but now it was in a poor state of repair. Nevertheless, it was just the sort of house Cheshire himself would have seized upon with both hands, and the idea caught on at once in this modest up-country town, in contrast to the great cities of London and Lagos, where the difficulties in the way of starting Homes seemed to be so much more daunting.

Among the Africans who saw the house that day and who caught the idea immediately was one of the two sons of the Chief Justice, who was at that time A.D.C. to the

Governor. He immediately caught the spirit of the venture, and when the party arrived back that afternoon in Freetown he hurried down to the docks, where his father was just arriving in a boat from England. He rushed on board, and told his astonished parent that he must positively take charge of a new Trust, which was to be established the next day.

Before Margot flew away on the morrow a Trust had been formed, and the first Trustees' meeting had been held. At this meeting several people were present who, nearly two years later, are still working hard for the Sierra Leone Homes—for there are now three of them, including two in Freetown. The Chief Justice presided, and is Chairman of the Foundation today. Others present were the new African Vice-Chancellor of Fourah Bay College, which now has the status of a university, several citizens of Freetown, and the wife of the Nigerian Commissioner, who herself had been one of the Trustees of the Nigerian Trust.

The group at Bo got down at once to cleaning and redecorating the house. Luckily we were able almost immediately to send May Cutler to them as the first matron. She had set the Home at Ibadan on its feet, and had fallen deeply in love with West Africa.

May Cutler is slight. You would think she would blow away in a strong wind. Like many small people, she has vitality of body and spirit out of proportion to her size. With Flora Tassell, she had breathed into the Children's Home at Ibadan a spirit of joy and happiness which will remain as long as the Home is there. Now, early in 1961, she stepped for the first time into the long, low house of Sir Milton Margai at Bo. It was not far from the road, and that was a good thing. It was also on the outskirts of the town, which was a good thing too, for she had no transport, and it would be easier for the helpers to visit the Home. There were two long rooms, with two smaller ones separating them. The long ones would be for the children, the smaller ones for whoever should be looking after them, or perhaps for a cook, and there was a little room near the entrance in which she put her handful of belongings.

The house was certainly in a pretty bad state, but that was only to be expected; and the roof looked as if it might fall down in a storm—in fact, a new one had to be put on. She had been two years in Nigeria, and she wondered about the rainy season, which, in fact, was only two months off. And, of course, there was the dirt, the desolation and the insects.

The committee now consisted of an energetic African surgeon, who had just come back to his own country from ten years' hard work in a Newcastle hospital. There was the wife of the Paramount Chief, who herself had been a nurse, the Mayor, the town magistrate, who had learned law from Professor Cheshire, and the wife of the manager of a business firm. The surgeon understood at once May Cutler's joy when she assessed with him the liabilities and assets of this empty house. The others were to understand, too, when they saw her move in with quiet determination to make the derelict house into a home.

Six months later I flew to Bo with the Permanent Secretary of one of the Ministries in Freetown, who was secretary to the newly formed Trust. We were met at the airport by the surgeon, who drove us at once to the Home. And there was May to meet us.

She looked even slighter than I had remembered, and rather pale; there was great joy in her face. The English administrator had told me in the aircraft flying up that the rains had been very severe—worse than he remembered them for many years. The Governor and his wife had been worried about May, as she had been cut off for those six months and had not been able to get away from the Home. We were both wondering how she had stood the ordeal. There was one consolation: the committee had just managed to get the new roof on before the rains had broken.

"Come in and see the children. We can have a cup of coffee and biscuits later on."

She got me by the sleeve and rushed us both into the first long room. There were seven beds in it, each one with a multi-coloured counterpane. The windows had gay curtains with a modern children's design.

"Now come out on to the veranda—the children are terribly excited."

There was a fairly large open space which jutted out from the veranda, a sort of *stoep*, and there were the seven little children in green rompers playing with their toys and as happy as children are anywhere when they are loved and cared for.

May Cutler gathered them in a circle round her. Some of them had to slide across the floor on their hands because their feet were disabled. Then they sang a song in their Mende language. The eldest was a girl of about ten. She was in a wheel-chair. She had sewn a pillow-case for Missy Mason on which she had embroidered a message. Would I take it to London?

We had coffee and biscuits with the committee in May's little room. She explained that they could take in more children, if they could only have more beds and mattresses. The Chief Justice had arranged for three more, which were on their way from Freetown, but that would only be enough for ten children and they could take seventeen.

"How much does a bed and mattress cost?" I asked.

"About seven pounds," was the bank manager's answer. Before leaving again for the airport—we had to catch the same plane on its return flight to Freetown—May Cutler showed me her accounts, which she was keeping in an exercise book. It was costing her committee about five shillings a week for each child. I was astonished, as I had been told that the cost of living in Sierra Leone, even in the districts, was not low.

"How on earth do you do it?" I asked her.

"I'll let you into a secret," she replied with a wink to the surgeon. "You see the kitchen window over there?"

"Yes," I replied. "It looks like any other kitchen window, except that it hasn't got any glass."

"It hasn't any glass and it faces on to the road. Once a week there's a whistle and when I go to the kitchen window, hey presto—there's a parcel of stuff on the window-sill from the cold store. One of the chaps there brings us milk and eggs he's paid for himself. And the Irish fathers give us all our flour."

Back in Freetown my administrator friend took me to two houses in Klinetown, in the railway colony near the sea beyond the docks. They were typical houses such as you can see in many parts of West Africa, built on stilts with an empty space beneath and access to the first floor by a covered staircase back and front. Sometimes they are called clapboard palaces.

"They aren't wanted any more by the railway, so we've managed to get them for the next Home here in Freetown on a peppercorn rent. Let's have a look at them. If you think they might be all right, I think we ought to get May Cutler down to see them. What do you think? Margot saw them in March and liked them."

They looked, as empty and deserted houses do look, unhappy and neglected. But they were just the thing for May Cutler.

Before I left the Chief Justice gave a party for us in his house. As far as I could see, every sort of person was there—Creoles, people from the interior, the old Protectorate, officials, Syrians and Lebanese, English people, Nigerians, men and women of all kinds and many countries. The Chief Justice spoke to me with affection of Lord Denning and Professor Cheshire. And then, as if by magic, the Governor's wife walked in with May Cutler. After they had been greeted by our host, the Governor's wife took me aside.

"We thought she needed a rest and a change, so we asked her to stay; she was brought down last night by road."

It was a wonderful climax to a memorable visit.

When I got back to London the bankers on the Finance Committee agreed to put up the overdraft by fifty pounds, so that seven more beds and mattresses could be bought at Bo.

In March, 1962, one year almost to a day after her first visit to Sierra Leone, Margot Mason landed once more at Lungi, and was flown across the wide expanse of water that separates from the mainland the island on which Freetown stands. Waiting to receive her as the plane landed was the Chief Justice. She could scarcely believe her eyes, for with him on the tarmac were two little children, their legs twisted and spindly, one on each side of May Cutler.

They took her off to see the new Home, the two houses in Klinetown standing in big compounds which had now been cleared by labour from the prison; and the next day the Freetown Cheshire Home was opened by Sir Milton Margai.

Only a month after all this had happened I was sitting on a bluff over the beautiful flamingo lake in the Manyara National Park in Tanganyika, on the other side of Africa. I had received a letter from Margot Mason describing the scene:

"There was an Army band playing in one corner of the compound; everybody was lined up in rows of chairs with their best hats on—I had to borrow mine—then the Prime Minister arrived and shook hands with us all. He was received by Johnny, the Chairman of the Home."

I remembered this tall African from my visit the previous September. He had been shot down in his Lancaster over Berlin during the winter of 1943, had landed by parachute in the snow, and had then spent some time in a German Air Force hospital after his capture. The trail of blood in the snow had led to the barn in which he had been hiding.

I went on reading the letter:

"Johnny went up the outside staircase of the house and made his little speech from the top step. I followed him with a pair of surgical scissors, and cut the tape which was stretched across the door. May came after me with the key on a cushion, followed by the Prime Minister, who opened the door. Out came the two little children, Babatundu and Mariattu. The Prime Minister made a speech, followed by the Chief Justice, who then left in a hurry to prepare a wonderful party which he gave for us all later in his house."

The letter ended with this sentence:

"At the end of the proceedings the house was blessed by the Muslim Divine, and by the Anglican and Roman Catholic Bishops."

Margot Mason flew on to Nigeria, where she lost no time in telling the people of Lagos that there was now an active Cheshire Home in Freetown.

The story of the Cheshire Homes in the Middle East, which is partly one of frustration and disappointment and partly one of success, perhaps belongs most logically to this chapter on Africa. For it was after her first trip to Nigeria in March, 1959, that Margot Mason flew on to Bethlehem, with the idea of seeing what could be done in the Middle East. This was a part of the world to which Cheshire had been powerfully attracted for a long time; he wanted to see what could be done to alleviate the great suffering and poverty in these countries.

Margot took with her the balance of her slender funds, £250, which had been sent to Market Mews over a period of several years, in small contributions, by the Kuwait Irish Society, against the time when it would be possible to start a Home in this part of the world.

Since the time of the New Testament the Arab world

has been a land where men are paramount. Its poverty and backwardness are due in no small degree to the unhappy and subservient position of Arab women. It was not the sort of situation into which an Englishwoman on her own could go with confidence, or with any assurance that she would receive encouragement in a task which was alien to the traditions of Arab life. And on this occasion not even Margot's hard work and will to succeed could overcome adverse local conditions.

She had been given a plan: it was to get started immediately whatever the cost. She decided to rent a house at once, and put into it several of the crippled children of whom Cheshire had been told in England. In those days part of her technique was to call on the resident representative of the United Kingdom. These hard-pressed officials wanted to be helpful, but often had as much difficulty in comprehending the inwardness of the Cheshire idea as people in less harassing surroundings at home. Her contacts with embassies and consulates were primarily for reconnaissance purposes—to find out who among the local people and the resident foreign communities, including the British, were likely to understand what she was getting at, and, having understood, to help actively in the work. The next prerequisite was that they should be able to co-operate with one another, even if they had never done so before and came, as they almost always did, from different national and cultural backgrounds.

The Consul-General in Jerusalem went out of his way to help. Before she could stop him, he telephoned a very important Arab on the other side of the frontier. His Excellency, as this V.I.P. styled himself, cannot have comprehended what this young foreigner woman was up to; nevertheless, he conducted her round his town, showing her properties for sale and for hire which she knew at once would be unsuitable, and which she sensed would be expensive.

Telling me about this tour afterwards, she described it in this way:

"To take the wind out of his sails, I quickly rented the first house I found to be faintly suitable. I knew then that it couldn't last very long, as we should soon outgrow it.

"Actually, the house was very nice. Not very large but light and airy, and with a beautiful view for miles across the fields in which the shepherds were when they saw the star. It had the advantage of being on the main road, and there were buses to Jerusalem and Bethlehem running by frequently."

I couldn't help wondering again at the confidence instilled by Cheshire.

"Didn't it seem an impossible task in that unpromising atmosphere?" I had asked her.

"Oh no!" she said gaily. "There were a few women at least—the men were not very helpful—and I knew that if I could only get some children in we should do the trick."

"Well, what happened?"

"I engaged an Arab nurse. I was told that she was the only fully trained one in town. We had a committee meeting of the women I had rounded up, who were inspired by the only Englishwoman at that time in Bethlehem. The first child was brought into the house that afternoon, at the same time as the first committee meeting was being held. The ladies were horrified to find that I had no blankets or sheets, but only a bare bedstead without a mattress. So they all disappeared to their homes and brought back one or two bits and pieces."

"What happened next?" I asked. "Did your Arab nurse turn up to help you?"

"Well, the next day a young boy came in who was mentally handicapped. I hadn't bargained for that, naturally. He slept all day and cried at night, and then the blow fell. The Arab nurse got ill and couldn't come, so I was on my own with the two children. A third was delivered unexpectedly the next morning by his grandfather. He was just dumped on the doorstep suffering from pneumonia. He had no resistance, being very undernourished, and died twelve hours after his grandfather left him on the doorstep."

She spent about ten days alone in the house with the two children, looking after them as best she could. Whenever she could get away she walked round Bethlehem, trying to bring a committee into existence. The English lady helped and encouraged her, but it was an impossible task.

"One of the troubles was that Arab men and women won't sit together, so I couldn't form the normal type of mixed committee."

She battled on, keeping the tiny Home going with one hand while trying to bring some sort of organization into being with the other. She managed to get away one day to Amman, the capital of Jordan. There she was able to gather together a few enthusiastic people, who also had some influence on opinion and affairs. She founded a Trust. The Vicar-General, who had read Cheshire's own book and those about him, took the lead, helped by the wife of the British Military Attaché to the King. An English girl, attached to the British Ambassy, helped in a most practical way, for she often motored up the winding hill to Bethlehem from the capital to be with the children in the Home, and so release Margot Mason to pursue the important objective of getting more people interested and setting up an administrative framework.

Margot stayed in Bethlehem for two months, and before she returned to England she arranged that Anne Thomas, matron of Seven Rivers, the Essex Home, should come out in due course to be the first permanent matron. Anne Thomas had been in the Cheshire movement from the early days, and had been matron of Alne

Hall, the first Home in the North. This was her first journey to the East, and she went in the tradition of Franciscan simplicity and courage. In London we saw to it that her insurance card was stamped regularly and that she was credited at the rate of two pounds a week for the work that she had undertaken to do.

When she arrived she found that the Home was not well regarded, for after Margot had left there had been a stop-gap appointment which had proved a failure. She put up with the same sort of loneliness that Margot Mason had known before her, but she had to bear it for a longer time, and this she did with fortitude. She stayed at Bethlehem for two years, and gathered into the Home a group of twenty disabled children. It became a happy Home, and it was the first in the Middle East.

Later in that year of 1960, Cheshire dropped in on his way to India. He had been there several times before; now he could no longer resist the pleas of the Trustees in Amman that a Home should be started there, where, they felt, there would be more support, more co-operation. He considered the problem, and agreed with them.

He wrote to me from Bombay about this visit:

"The Bethlehem Home is beautifully run, and just before I left for Beirut the Prime Minister called to see it. If ever there were doubts of any sort at all about the general set-up, all is well now, and I think a great opportunity lies ahead. Do you think you could do your utmost to help as quickly as possible?"

And so another project started in this country. The Home at Amman began in the usual way; there was no intention on the part of either Cheshire or Margot Mason that it should replace the children's Home at Bethlehem, but the Government became interested, a plot of land was given by King Hussein, who had said that he hoped a rehabilitation centre would be built by the Jordan Trust on the site, and the committee felt that two Homes would be beyond their strength. None of them in Amman nor yet any of us in London, when we heard of the decision to build this centre at the capital, had any idea where the money would come from. Then, two days after I had read out Cheshire's cable to my banker friends on the Finance Committee, we had a letter from a solicitor in Blackpool saying that a client of his had recently died and had bequeathed three thousand pounds to Group Captain Cheshire personally, to be used in any way he thought fit. As time went on considerable sums of money, in addition to this legacy, were sent to Jordan.

The fortunes of the Amman Home are an example of Cheshire's excessive optimism, for, as in some other cases, he had not looked sufficiently far below the surface. Great opportunities do lie ahead in this area, which is so close to his heart, but so far the venture at Amman has eluded his control and is far from being in the spirit of simplicity and poverty which is so important to him—simply because the cost of building, as in most countries, seemed to rise during construction in a way that made us feel that the project was getting out of our control.

A year later Alderman Jack Stephens, who had been Mayor of Penzance when St. Teresa's began, was present when the King laid the foundation stone. When the new Home is ready, the little Children's Home in Bethlehem, which had inspired the more ambitious project in Amman, will probably disappear. But Cheshire himself has no intention of leaving Bethlehem for good.

CHAPTER TEN

VIEW FROM A WHEEL-CHAIR

MEANWHILE, WHAT WAS life like in the Homes in England? We have an interesting testimony at this period from Ginger Farrell, victim of multiple sclerosis, whose history has been given in an earlier chapter. He was normally resident at Heatherley in Sussex, but he travelled round to most of the Homes, spending a fortnight or so in each, long enough to become part of the Home and a friend of the patients. The pleasure he derived from the sights and sounds of the countryside on his travels between the Homes reflects another longing of the disabled, most of whom are chained to their beds and wheel-chairs.

He described to me a visit to two of the northern Homes:

"The weather was perfect. We went over the Pennines and the moors, where we passed through the Brontë country. The Home we were making for was at the side of a main road which ran north. It was about a hundred years old, set in the middle of beautiful gardens, surrounded by meadows in which sheep and cattle were grazing."

"Could you tell me something of what it was like living in a Home?" I asked.

"Well, here again, as always, I felt like a new boy at school. There was a very imposing entrance, but because of the steps and my invalid chair I was taken to the back, where a ramp made my entrance easy. We came through the lounge, and I was struck by the tranquil air. What a different set of people these were from those in another Home I had visited recently! They were quieter, more thoughtful, and their welcome seemed to me to come from their hearts."

I think this statement made me realize for the first time that each of the Homes must have a sort of corporate personality which is more clearly evident to the people who themselves live in one of the Cheshire Homes than to outsiders. And it was during this talk that I made the rather obvious discovery that the community in each Home must to some extent reflect the broad divisions of the community outside.

"Can you distinguish between different types of patients?" I asked.

"Some of them," he went on, "have been ill from birth or from early youth. These cope extremely well, because children are skilful in adapting their lives to any disabilities. They seem to be more resilient than those who are hit in their teens or middle-age. They don't seem to regret the normal life they might have had. The other half of the patients in each Home, speaking generally, will have spent twenty or thirty years of ordinary living, with a normal career, before being struck down, and it is these who have the hardest job of readjustment. Many do it well, but there is a small residue who can never make the adjustment and who carry a large chip on their shoulder, facing life with the 'Why did this have to happen to me?' attitude."

Then he went back to the Home he had liked so much in the North of England.

"I stayed quite a time there, and in a few weeks got to know the patients a lot better, and some of the staff and the management committee, too. I heard of the time at the start of the Home when it had many trials and difficulties. This isn't uncommon, as you know only too well. We've had them here at Heatherley, and we shall go on having them, I'm sure. It usually takes three or four years before the major problems are ironed out and a Home settles down."

I was a bit worried that this long talk would tire him, but he seemed so much better since his operation at the National Hospital. He and Pamela Farrell were the inspiration of this new Home in Sussex, which she had conjured out of the air within a year with the devotion and enthusiasm particularly of the people of Crawley, but also of the whole county of Sussex. It has become a true home, not only for her husband and herself, but for thirty-seven disabled men and women.

"Can you give me some idea from the inside, as it were, of the others in that northern Home?" I asked.

"Yes, I remember my feelings so well, as I looked round the dining table at the dozen patients. 'What a mockery of human behaviour this is!' was my first reaction, as I saw them struggling with their food. I suppose I looked just as bad to them.

"On my left was David, a man of fifty, who had suffered from muscular dystrophy since his early teens. For some time he had been able to earn a living, but for the last eight years he has been in a wheel-chair. He was able to feed himself by means of the initial flourish of the shoulder-blades leading to slow movements of the hands, which is so typical of this disease. David was one of the few Roman Catholics in the Home. This seemed to sustain him, for he was a happy and cheerful man. He had a business head and ran the shop. Next to him was a middle-aged woman who had been a schoolmistress teaching Latin in a big girls' school. She had an appalling piece of luck on a visit to Oxford, when she fell down a couple of steps in the gloom of one of the colleges and broke two bones in her neck, which paralysed the rest of her body. Strength was slowly returning to her limbs."

And so it had gone on. Two brothers with Parkinson's disease, a beautiful girl with multiple sclerosis, a middle-aged woman with rheumatoid arthritis. Somehow it all sounded pretty grim, and I said so.

"No, it isn't, at least not from the point of view I think

you mean. You see, here at Heatherley—and I think it's pretty well the same at most of the Homes—we are all living at the rate of five thousand a year. If we want an extra TV set we get it at once; if we want a new appliance, we get it." And he pointed to a new gadget on the bed by his chair, a kind of sling, which made it easier for him to turn the pages of a book or newspaper by holding up his forearm.

"If we want to get about more in the countryside, we are given a bus with the seats taken out and adapted to take our wheel-chairs and appliances."

He paused and screwed up his face. I was worried that something had happened, but he was only concentrating. He went on:

"But you need more than this, just as people outside with five thousand a year need more."

His wife joined in the conversation now. She had come into the room and had been listening to the last part of our talk.

"It's terribly hard to say, of course, but I think they do become better people in a Cheshire Home. At least, that's what we feel after nearly a year here—that is, the people who were basically good before they were ill. Some may not have been so on the surface and it has taken adversity to bring out their moral stamina, because, you know, they do give out something to us healthy people, and it's rather wonderful."

She was speaking with the conviction of someone who knew absolutely what she was talking about. I was sure she was not thinking of her husband at that moment, but that they were both thinking as a team about their patients. Looking quietly at him, I felt that here was the supreme example, perhaps, in all the Cheshire Homes of a disabled man who gave strength to everyone who came within the radius of his wheel-chair. I certainly felt it strongly throughout our talk. He was a man who had been brave enough to admit during a broadcast talk that he had almost committed suicide when he found he could not continue with his practice, but that his faith in God had given him the strength to turn back at the last moment from his own drug cupboard.

Then they both spoke of the vital need to have temperamentally compatible people in a Home. It was always best, they thought, to arrange for a period of trial for both sides, the patient and the Home. This might sound callous, but in the long run it was better to have a happy community; and they emphasized that this did not by any means involve turning down the heavier nursing cases, for the heaviness of the nursing did not necessarily have anything to do with the temperament and spirit of the patient; in fact, the worst afflicted were often the strongest characters who would contribute the most to the Home and its happiness.

Later in this same summer I flew over to Ireland, at Cheshire's request, to represent him at the opening of the first Home there, as he had suddenly fallen ill from a disease which took some time to diagnose. It turned out to be a kind of sprue, which he had originally contracted in India and had not got rid of. He was ordered to bed and then to rest for twelve months.

Ardeen, the house on the Cullatin Estate among the lovely hills of County Wicklow, had been given by Lady Fitzwilliam, who lived in the big Georgian house a mile away. She and her sister had been the driving force behind this new Home, which was to be opened in June, 1962. It had experienced its full measure of headaches and crises, and was to be opened now by Mr. MacEntee, the Minister of Health and Deputy Prime Minister of Eire. As on so many other occasions, I found it hard to believe my eyes as I sat behind Mr. MacEntee on the little wooden platform which the committee had set up outside the drawing-room of the house. On the lawn below, which sloped away to a field, there were gathered about a thousand people, many of them from Dublin, sixty miles away. Dotted among the crowd were the wheel-chairs of the fifteen patients, a few of them lying full-length, for this Home had already taken in at least four very heavy cases. Among the crowd, too, there were Irish soldiers in khaki battle-dress, for there had been a guard of honour for the Minister to inspect when he had arrived; and, of course, there were Pressmen and photographers. But the main thing was the atmosphere of happiness, and a sort of corporate feeling of achievement. It had really come off, and who, even among the committee and their helpers, had believed this would be possible even a month before? I think for me this is the magic of it all, for even if you have seen it happen time after time, both in England and in the most unlikely places abroad, every time it happens again there seems to be something miraculous about the process.

In my speech I told them a little of the Cheshire story in West Africa, as this seemed appropriate, in view of Ireland's recent contribution to the difficult situation in the Congo. I told them about Cheshire's illness, and how sad he was not to be with them, and at the same time that it was this same illness which had prevented him from paying his first trip to West Africa to visit the Homes in Sierra Leone and Nigeria, none of which he had yet seen, though there were now eight of them. The Irish, too, belonged to the select band of people who had succeeded in starting a Home without his personal help and inspiration, although he had been able to make one or two public appearances in Dublin.

After the speeches were over Mr. MacEntee cut a tape which had been stretched across the french window of the drawing-room, and the Home was formally opened. It was just after this that I was introduced to Joan Horan.

She is a handsome woman with dark hair, and although she sits in a wheel-chair, paralysed from the waist downwards, there is that something about her which tells you she is a smart woman. She looked radiantly happy, and asked me if I would like to have tea with her in her room. I accepted her invitation, and when tea had been brought in we settled down to talk.

"You look so very happy," I said. "I hope you don't mind my mentioning it, but it's so striking."

"Well, you see, I am tremendously happy. For the first time for what seems like an age, I feel I have a home of my own."

"Could you tell me how it all happened?" I asked her.

"Of course I will, and perhaps you'll be able to explain then to Group Captain Cheshire how immensely grateful I feel to him for having inspired people in Ireland to start this Home, where by some amazing chance I've been able to find a home myself after years of living in hospital wards, and for quite a lot of them face downwards."

Joan Horan was born in Dublin in 1918, in one of the Georgian houses on Merrion Square, where the doctors used to live. Her father had been a surgeon. When she was still a little girl the family had moved to a large house in the suburbs where there had been a garden and a tennis court. Her family were fond of games, and she soon became a good tennis-player and a keen swimmer. When she was seventeen she decided to become an actress, and spent three happy years at the Central School of Dramatic Art. But, like many other stage-struck girls, she found it hard to get anything more rewarding than small parts in plays or crowd scenes in films.

"My father had been quite right—I was not cut out to be an actress. But those four years taught me a lot, and hardened me for many things which were to happen in the future."

She married when she was twenty-three, and settled down in Dublin. There were two boys, but the marriage was not successful, and after nine years she obtained a legal separation from her husband, with the custody of her younger son. It was just before this upheaval in her life that she first had an inkling of the physical breakdown that was so tragically to strike her in the full flush of a healthy and vigorous life. She developed a cyst in her back which pressed on the main nerve column in her spine. She had an operation and then, as money was short and she had to have a job, she came over to England. She did a number of things during this uncertain period: she was a housekeeper-companion in Somerset, a barmaid at a pub, and then a farm help. During this time she started to lose the power of her right leg, and the girl who had been such a good tennis-player and swimmer found that she couldn't even run. Soon it even became difficult to go up and down stairs. In her precarious position it was a frightening development.

I watched the strong, attractive face and listened to her story, told with the lightest of Irish brogues, as we drank our tea. Through the window of her room I could see the drive and all the bustle of the guests, who were beginning to leave. She went on with her story:

"I returned to Dublin and had a second spinal operation. After that I could only hobble with the help of a stick—one ruckle in the carpet and I fell flat on my face. So that was the end of work for me, and the finish of most of the things I loved, like dancing, driving a car, seeing my friends and leading an active life."

She made a great effort to organize a life for her son, so that he could be with her at least during his school holidays. She took a small flat with a garden, and her son did all the shopping, but it was not to last, as the doctors said she must have another operation on her spine. This time she went into the National Hospital in Queen's Square in London, of which our Trustee, Cherry Morris, with whom this book began, was the head almoner.

"It was March, 1953, and little did I know when I was

carried on to the plane at Dublin airport that it would be seven years before I should be travelling sitting up in an aircraft again."

She was to spend two and a half years at the National Hospital lying flat on her stomach. Her memories of that grim period were of the kindnesses shown to her by many people, the nurses taking her shopping on her trolley, the policeman who used to hold up the traffic, the firm which fixed special footplates to her wheel-chair and even made a special trolley to her own design which she propelled around in her prone position. And then she said something which repeated almost word for word what Ginger Farrell had said to me at Heatherley:

"I don't think I could point to a day, a time or any special event when it dawned on me that I would never walk again; it just seemed to settle on me and I took it for granted. It's difficult to feel sorry for yourself when you are in hospital with so many much more tragic cases than your own."

She was transferred back to a hospital in Dublin, and there were serious doubts as to whether she would live. But she clearly had the will to live, and in 1958 she went on a pilgrimage to Lourdes, where she received the same kind of spiritual uplift at the sight of so many others in worse plight than herself as Cheshire had in 1954. The trip did not bring her a cure, but it gave her an inspiration which has remained with her to the present day.

Then came the decisive moment in her new life—that life which seemed destined to be passed in an unending series of hospital wards with their constant "hallos" and "goodbyes". They seemed to her to be like the airports of this world, except that she was always the one who stayed behind looking on at events from her restricted position, while the others went on their journeys to the world outside.

"In 1959 I had the wonderful luck to go to Stoke Mandeville Hospital in England, where the motto is pretty well 'Do or die.' I had to do things by myself that I had never been set to do since I was first ill, and after a lot of violent physiotherapy I found myself sitting up in a wheel-chair after only one month there. After six years of lying on my tummy, it seemed like a dream to look at things the right way up again. The first thing I did was to wheel over to the wash-basin and wash my hands in running water. It was wonderful."

Every summer at Stoke Mandeville they hold their own international games for the patients. Joan Horan's early history as an athletic girl was known to the staff, and they were determined that she should try to play some game which might be within her limited but growing powers. So in July, 1959, she was lowered gently into the pool to represent Ireland in the swimming events, the only member of the Irish team. To her amazement, she found that she could do the crawl and the breast stroke as well as ever, and she won two gold medals.

After a period at Stoke Mandeville, she had to go back to the hospital at Dublin, which was depressing after the stimulus of the great hospital in Buckinghamshire. Then came the second interlude, another lightening of the sky. In September, 1960, an Irish team of five disabled men and women in wheel-chairs was sent to Rome, where an Olympic meeting for the disabled of the world was held after the main games were over.

"It was a wonderful thrill to fly over the Alps, my first flight since that sad day in 1953 when I left Dublin airport for the National Hospital in London. We stayed in the Olympic village for eight days. One of the most wonderful experiences was to be present when His Holiness Pope John gave an audience to the disabled athletes, all six hundred of us in wheel-chairs."

She won no less than two gold medals for Ireland—the swimming and the archery—and had the extraordinary experience, for someone who is paralysed below the waist, of being wheeled on to a Victory rostrum at an international gathering and hearing the strains of her own National Anthem being played and watching her own national flag waving in the breeze for herself and her achievements. She went back to the hospital in Dublin, and it was then she heard that a Cheshire Home might be starting up in Ireland.

"Like a shot from a gun, I headed for the lady almoner's office, and I think I must have been the first patient on the list."

As bad luck would have it, just when the Ardeen Home was ready to take its first patients Joan Horan had to have another operation, which kept her in hospital for a further three months, so she missed the chance of being in the first four. But at last the day came, and she was taken by car, with all her belongings, to the house on the hill near the village of Shillelagh in the beautiful green hills of County Wicklow.

"I won't say I wasn't nervous, because I was—not only nervous, but scared to death of what lay ahead. Should I like it? Would the staff be able to manage me, or should I be too much bother?"

These thoughts troubled her all the way down from Dublin, as they were bound to do, for she had experienced so many disappointments and, despite her remarkable recovery and achievements, she was still a heavy case which even the hospitals found difficult enough. It was not at all unlikely that a Cheshire Home, which she knew was not a hospital, might find her altogether too much trouble, with the result that she would find herself back again in the dreary and so familiar surroundings of the hospital wards, with their unending "hallos" and "goodbyes", the heartache and the boredom.

"I needn't have worried. As soon as I saw the house in the distance standing up there on the hill, somehow I felt it was going to be all right. When we arrived at the front door I was welcomed as if I were coming home, as indeed I was. It's almost impossible to put into words what this lovely house means to me. The peace and quiet, after nine years of ward life, is unbelievable."

She had brought to Ardeen her bows and arrows, but she had no backing for the face of her target. In no time the committee had arranged for six bales of straw—out of season—and she was able to sit in the garden in her chair and carry on with one of the sports at which she excelled, and which she could do with grace and success, despite her disability. She soon had a little electric poker, and with her artistic sense, which had not been killed by the pain and the suffering of the years, she produced a series of designs on wood which found ready buyers and added to the patients' fund.

She was to cross over to England again for the Stoke Mandeville games this summer. She won no more gold medals, but it didn't worry her at all. She came back to Ardeen to a welcome from the patients, the staff and the local friends of the Home which was deep and warm.

We had finished our tea and I got up to go. Her parting words were:

"Now I can settle down again in the beauty of the Wicklow Hills, the peace of the Irish countryside, and enjoy to the full all the things that go to make up a happy family, the laughs, the occasional tears, and above all the wonderful feeling of love and security."

As I paused at the door to say goodbye she said to me quietly:

"Will you tell Group Captain Cheshire when you next see him how grateful I am to him? What more could I ask? I thank him from the bottom of my heart."

CHAPTER ELEVEN

THE BIRTH OF AN IDEA

AT THIS STAGE of the story we must go back a few years, to the winter of 1957–8, when Cheshire was on his third visit to India. Soon after Christmas some notes came into Market Mews on a tape from Jamshedpur, the Tata steel town in eastern India. On this tape was the germ of an idea that has become, in five years, an important element of the whole movement. Played back in the sitting-room of Margot Mason's little house in Market Mews it didn't at first sound very revolutionary:

"I want you to send out a memorandum, Dopey, to all the Trustees so that they can think about it before they meet. The idea is to set up a Home—a sort of international unit—which will not be under any national foundation. It will take the heavy nursing cases which the other Homes won't take, and it will train people who are dedicated to the work, people who once they are qualified will go out to different parts of the world to found their own Homes or to do whatever may be needed. I think this international Home should be in India, because India stands between the East and the West, and is a bridge between them."

Cheshire always spoke in the future tense when he was putting up a new scheme, for there was never doubt in his own mind but that his plan was already halfway to realization. Although I had become used to this technique, I didn't really take in what he was saying at this first hearing. Homes all over the world . . . the vista of many lights which he had spoken about to Frances Jeram in the Peacock room at Le Court. Did he really see this happening? What did make an impact, however, was the reference to the fact that as the Homes multiplied committees were beginning to show reluctance to take in the heavier nursing cases—the ones Arthur Dykes had said Cheshire must accept, if he accepted all sizes of cheques, the cases which Frances Jeram and the patients themselves had never refused at the old Le Court.

So Margot Mason sat down to work out the memorandum, and Lord Denning started the discussion at the Trustees' meeting a month later. Since we could no longer meet in his office, our gatherings now took place in the sitting-room at Market Mews. Most of the chairs had no springs, and there were no carpets on the floor.

I don't think any of us really believed that this idea of an international unit was practical politics, although it sounded exciting and made us more aware than we had been that Cheshire was actually achieving something in those distant places to which he disappeared so often. Until this meeting in the winter of 1958 I had been the only Trustee who had been in India, and certainly the only one to have seen a Cheshire Home in action outside England, but now his father was also able to speak with first-hand knowledge. He and Mrs. Cheshire had spent the winter in India visiting the six Homes which were in operation. He was able to explain the difficulty inherent in his son's new plan.

"Larry Donnelly, the chap who is running the show in Calcutta, and has done so much for Leonard, isn't happy about the idea of an institution which doesn't come under the Indian Foundation, especially if it is to be set up at Jamshedpur, where the local people want a Home that is purely local and under their own control."

Donnelly had been Managing Trustee of the Indian Foundation for two critical years and had built up remarkable support in Calcutta for the Home there, Serampore. I could well believe that he would resist any attempt to start a new organization in India, yet outside the control of the Indian Foundation.

What had forced Cheshire to look for such a headquarters were the many opportunities for his work which seemed to him to be presenting themselves in different countries, and the realization that he could no longer deal with them personally. He wanted to be everywhere, and, since that was impossible, he realized that the next best thing was to work through the medium of other people who understood completely what he was trying to do, and were imbued with the same ideals as he was himself, so that he could rely on them to carry on independently. If this was to be accomplished, some process of training was necessary. Individual Homes with their own committees and their own affairs could not in his view reflect at all times the ideas and objectives of the movement as a whole. So he needed a personal headquarters which would also be a training unit, and to which would come not only future founders of Homes but the staff from existing Homes for refresher courses.

It was this feeling which in 1957 had taken him in the first instance to Bihar, where someone had told him of a property which sounded suitable. He went off from Calcutta to look at it with Larry Donnelly, stopping on the way at Jamshedpur for the night. When he woke up in the morning he was struck by the beauty of the place—a strange feeling to have about a steel town. But in fact the Tata family, who built it out of the jungle, have made it a beautiful township with its planned streets, its gardens and hospitals and lakes, a model for the industrial complexes of both East and West. Cheshire decided to investigate the property situation there. It didn't seem very hopeful in a town where 90 per cent. of the land was owned by the Company, and exorbitantly expensive. However, by a lucky chance he was put in touch with a Father of the American Jesuit Mission, who spent an entire afternoon driving him round from one property to another, finally ending up at an estate some five miles out of the city, called the Rustomji J. Patel estate.

As they walked across the railway line through the rusty iron gates and up the gravelled drive towards the strongly built, attractive bungalow, the sun was setting and darkness falling. As far as the eye could see there were fruit trees, flowering shrubs and occasional towering limes. It was a veritable oasis of peace and beauty in a parched and dusty countryside, and Cheshire knew that he had found what he was looking for. When the Jesuit told him that the thirty-five-acre estate had been given to the Order on the understanding that it should be used for children in need, and that he could have it if he agreed to the condition, he accepted—but only after some hesitation, for children were an entirely new departure, and he wanted to be sure that he was not being false to his mission.

In the months that followed he was to devote the greater part of his time and energy to the task of building the estate up jointly as a home for crippled children and his international centre. But it was not to prove easy, and little, if anything, went according to plan.

In the first place, he was due to return to England with no time to form a committee in Jamshedpur before he left. Then one day a roving Englishman who was moving round the world on his own volunteered to take over the estate and start getting the premises habitable so that they could take in crippled children from Calcutta and Jamshedpur. After the usual shaky start, with very little in the way of nursing help, one of the most remarkable of the many women who were to help Cheshire in his work arrived on the scene from Australia.

Lesley Reardon, who was a trained nurse and had been working in the outback, had heard of Cheshire's work in England and India, and had written to him to say that she would like to volunteer to nurse in one of his

Homes in India, without salary. Her arrival marked the turning-point in this Home, which, largely because of its doubtful start, had lost the confidence of the people of Jamshedpur. Lesley Reardon pulled it round, and public confidence grew. Sadly, this remarkable Australian girl contracted a disease which the local doctors were not able to diagnose. She went into hospital, and died after a short time.

The committee of this Home, which was now more confident of the future, nevertheless objected strongly to the whole idea of an international centre. They could understand a children's Home, and could see the responsibilities which this might involve for them; they would not consider something additional and strange which might result in unforeseen and unforeseeable commitments. But Cheshire himself, in addition to his own strong convictions, could not forget that Lesley Reardon had backed up his idea before her death, and had been in favour of using the estate to the maximum of its potentiality.

His certainty was strengthened by something which happened towards the end of 1957, when he visited the Government Hospital at Sindhri, north-east of Jamshedpur. He was introduced to a young man of twenty-five who had fallen off a factory roof and broken his back, and whom the hospital were going to discharge even though he was paralysed from the waist down and had a superpubic tube. Though the boy and Cheshire could not talk to one another, a look of understanding passed between them—from the one a silent, frightened appeal for help, from the other a promise that something would be done. It was as if the voice of old Arthur Dykes was calling from the paddy fields of Bihar. But this was one promise at least that was never fulfilled, one call that was never answered, for the opposition of the committee at Jamshedpur was unyielding. Jamshedpur, they said, was for children, not for adults; it was a Home, not a hospital, and to take so serious and heavy a nursing case would be an act of irresponsibility, a violation of medical commonsense. So the boy was returned to his village, three miles off the nearest dirt road. In desperation Cheshire turned for help to the Mission to Lepers, who sent an expedition to rescue the boy, only to find that he had died a few days after his arrival home, apparently of poisoning—which proved, if indeed it needed proving, that the argument, "We are not sufficiently well equipped to take a man like that," has no validity when there is nowhere better to send him.

So violent and ungiving was the resistance to his idea of combining the children's Home and the international centre that Cheshire was undoubtedly shaken. Left to himself he might well have hesitated to force the issue, for fear of wilfully flying in the face of Providence. But his conviction of the need for such a centre was strengthened by the support of his father and mother when they came to India to visit all the six Homes, and to see for themselves what their son had achieved. As it turned out, the tour was to make a major stage in the history of the Indian Foundation, for Professor Cheshire, who either at Oxford or at Lincoln's Inn had lectured to many of the leading lawyers and politicians in the land, and whose books were sold and used all over the English-speaking world, was better known to the people who mattered in India than his son. At nearly every stop he was fêted, and in consequence the Homes became more widely known. But the outstanding achievement of the visit was undoubtedly the support which both parents gave to their son's idea, believing, as they did, that he must have at least one Home where he was free, where he could work as he once did at Le Court.

Then and there Cheshire packed his bag, handed over to the local committee the vehicles and equipment which he had laboriously accumulated at Jamshedpur for his international centre, and left for Dehra Dun, 1,000 miles to the north-west, not knowing at all how his idea would be received there, but seeing no alternative.

In Dehra Dun he had found the local committee of the Home, all of whom were Indians, reluctant to go against what they considered to be the wishes of the Trustees in Calcutta, Bombay and Delhi, but sympathetic enough to give him shelter in their house and to be willing to try and work out some means of helping him. Their first suggestion was to turn their own Home into the international one, but this would have meant administering it through a committee, which it was his object to avoid. So they agreed to let him use the derelict top floor of the Home as his personal base, and establish his centre wherever he could find suitable land. I think this was an important moment; certainly it was a brave decision by the committee, and one for which Cheshire has never ceased to be grateful.

It was not until several years later that I realized how lonely he was at this time, and what comfort and strength he had drawn from his father's and mother's visit. Now they had left India, clearly the worse in health for their tour, he felt that he had exposed them to too much worry and fatigue. Relations with Donnelly were strained. The local committee's loyalty was clearly being stretched to the limit. He was without funds, and apparently without the possibility of acquiring any, since he had no means of appealing for money outside the various Foundations themselves. However, his experience at Jamshedpur had taught him that at all costs he must have a centre where he could take needy and urgent cases not acceptable to the Homes. Dehra Dun, moreover, with the foothills of the Himalayas rising ten miles away, was a splendid place for peaceful thought and contemplation.

There appeared to be two possibilities for a site. One was to buy a large open space on the near side of the Rispana River, where power and water would be available from the town supply, but which would cost a fair amount of money and had little in the way of beauty to commend it. The other was to negotiate for some forest land on the far side of the river, which was unbelievably beautiful and secluded compared with the drabness of the city land, and free from the prospect of being ultimately enclosed within a residential area. The trouble was that it had no services at all. There was no chance of drilling for water on this site, since no water existed there—even the town of Dehra Dun was short of water. Nobody believed that the Corporation would give him water for an organization situated outside the city limits. Corporation outlooks are much the same the world over.

Once again there was the determined yet relaxed approach to the target. Once again it was the beauty of the natural surroundings which had already decided him to plump for the more difficult proposition—the beauty and the privacy.

At the next meeting of the English Trustees, in July, 1958, we had the story from Cheshire himself.

"What will you call this new institution?" Lord Denning asked him.

"Sue Ryder and I thought we would call it Raphael."

This was the first time he had mentioned to the Trustees the woman who was later to become his wife, though they had first met at Ampthill three years ago on a cold and dreary afternoon, when he was getting ready to go to India. Sue Ryder had suddenly become well-known at this time to the many millions of people in Britain who watch television, although she had devoted herself to the stateless and disabled survivors of the Nazi concentration camps ever since the war, and already had numbers of supporters up and down the country. After this first visit to Ampthill she used to come over quite often, bringing parties of her refugees with her. When Staunton Harold started up she paid several visits there too; in fact, she and her Polish friends reconstructed the back courtyard. In those days this slightly built but determined girl was something of an enigma to Cheshire, since he couldn't understand how she managed to keep going with such furious energy; not did he have an inkling of the size of the problems which confronted her. She was so immersed in her work that she had little time or inclination to explain to others what she was trying to do.

At the beginning of the war, when she was still only sixteen, she had managed to join Special Forces, the organization responsible for sending agents in and out of occupied Europe. She was seconded to the Polish Section, and there she learnt at first-hand of the full horror of the Nazi occupation, a knowledge which has always remained with her, and still drives her unceasingly in her determination to help those who suffered under a tyranny unparalleled in the history of mankind. Inspired by the courage and cheerfulness of the Poles in the face of wholesale torture and extermination, she pledged herself to repay in some small measure, as much as one individual could, something of the debt which she considered those who had never known a German occupation owed to their less fortunate Allies. And this she has done.

The story of Sue Ryder's work and the Forgotten Allies Trust, as the organization is called which she founded to help them, is a book in itself. Here it is only possible to touch upon the kind of person who was to play such a large part in the building up of Raphael. Faced with the sometimes heartbreaking task of befriending and caring for Europe's homeless, she set herself with all her might, and with the great patience and compassion with which she is blessed, to make them feel that they were not in fact just forgotten allies. Averaging less than four hours a night in bed—sometimes going nights on end with no sleep at all—and existing through force of circumstances and poverty on little more than soup, biscuits and coffee, she drove the length and breadth of Germany, visiting the camps, the hospitals and the prisons, bringing a personal service which, even if it was not large in relation to the problem, restored hope and self-respect to more people than will ever be known. Undaunted by the opposition which she sometimes encountered in England, and supported by the band of loyal helpers which she was gradually building up, she laid the foundations of what was to become a unique organization.

It was not surprising, then, that when Cheshire needed a partner to help him set up his international centre he should turn to Sue Ryder. The centre, after all, was intended not only to take the emergency and difficult cases that the local Homes would not or could not accept, but to counteract what seemed to him the shortcomings inherent in his own Foundation. If it were managed by people chosen from the Foundation itself, however devoted they might be, would not the centre of necessity reflect the very flaws which it was designed to eradicate? In Cheshire's eyes, what he needed was someone who had personal experience of what it was to start something up from scratch, with no one on whom to lean other than the Providence of God. The two organizations, his and Sue's, could, he felt, by some form of collaboration help one another to strengthen and grow. Sue's was a personal work which did not easily lend itself to delegation or administration; it had the spirit, but not a strong organizational framework. The Cheshire Foundation, on the other hand, had its Trustees, its committees, its rules of procedure, but for that very reason was in danger of losing its spirit. Some form of association might well be of great value to both movements. But the point was—how?

Meanwhile, at the very moment when Cheshire was settling down to his task of founding his international centre, Sue Ryder was setting out on one of her most adventurous missions—to see if anything could be done for the survivors of Nazism in Poland itself. In those days entry into any of the Eastern European countries was difficult in the extreme, and she went, driving alone in her small, aged car, without any kind of official backing or any introductions or contacts. In the ten days which she spent in Poland she visited a dozen or so hospitals, saw something of the immense need of the sick in a country in which 1,800 hospitals had been systematically destroyed during the war, and persuaded the Deputy Minister of Health to convene a conference of doctors and other officials to discuss the whole problem. The conference, after a difficult start, ended by deciding that any help she could give would be very welcome, and invited her to return as soon as possible in order to draw up a formal agreement and so put her plan on to a proper footing. Thus was opened another door on the road towards Sue's and Cheshire's common goal of expanding their work to different countries of the world. In the light of this, the international centre clearly took on an altogether new significance.

The impact of all this on the English Trustees was, to say the least of it, unsettling. They had just got over the shock of Cheshire's first adventure overseas. To most people's surprise, things had gone remarkably well. Now, just as we had begun to get used to the idea of periodic absences from England, he planned to team up with a girl who seemed to be the counterpart of himself in another field, but who was clearly going to submit her work to no outside authority.

Whatever doubts the Trustees had about this new development, Cheshire himself had none, as he made clear in a conversation with Lady Denning.

"The time has come," she said to him, "when you must decide between one single organization controlled in England by a Board of Trustees and a Chairman, and a series of unco-ordinated enterprises each capable of going its own way. I strongly advise the former—otherwise you will be divided against yourself."

"Yes, I see all that," Cheshire replied, "but actually I have a different solution. I'm convinced that the right thing is to team up with Sue Ryder, though at the moment we neither of us see quite how it is to be done. A single organization means putting a lot of power in the hands of one person, and sooner or later it may attract the wrong person. It means high overheads and all the drawbacks of bureaucracy, which will slowly kill the personal basis on which the work was founded. Worse still, an organization run from London is not likely to be acceptable in the Far East, where my chief sympathies lie, and would make it fundamentally impossible to bring in the Communist bloc on an equal footing with us, which is my goal just as it is Sue's. She will concentrate on Eastern Europe and Russia, because of her long association with them, and I on China and the Far East. Together we can strengthen and improve each other, and together we can run the international settlements which are the principal means of perpetuating the spirit of the work with a free hand, unhampered by trusts and committees."

To some of us, inevitably, this whole conception of a world-wide movement seemed like a dream of Utopia. But in the next few years Cheshire and Sue Ryder were to put their combined energy into taking the first steps to turn the dream into reality.

CHAPTER TWELVE

RAPHAEL

November, 1958, marked the beginning of this new and revolutionary phase. As Cheshire had told the Trustees at the meeting in the summer, they had decided on a name for the Indian Settlement. It was to be Raphael, after the Archangel, one of the Seven who stand in the presence of God, and who escorted the young Tobias on his long journey from Ecbatana to Rages and back, saved him from many dangers, brought him peace and happiness, and finally cured his father's blindness. In addition to their normal activities, Sue and Cheshire had by this time each seen more of the other's work; and they now set off severally on their respective missions—Sue to build up her Polish Foundation, Cheshire to try to launch Raphael in India.

A new development took place shortly after his arrival in Dehra Dun. He was taken by the parish priest—an Italian Franciscan—to visit the lepers in the "Dip." It was an extraordinary and moving experience. The "Dip" was three-quarters of an acre of ground, much like a quarry in appearance, and adjacent to the city refuse dump. There, in closely crowded mud huts, lived some hundred and fifty leprosy patients, all beyond cure, some still infective, most of them married. Because of the presence in the neighbourhood of a small but good leprosarium, they had come down over the years from the surrounding hills, hoping for a cure. By the time they had discovered that a cure was not possible they were afraid to return to their villages, where in any case their fast-growing deformities would have made them unwelcome, and so they stayed in Dehra Dun, living on the streets, or under the trees, or wherever they could find an undisturbed corner. In due course a sympathetic Chairman of the Municipal Council had given them the "Dip" in which to make themselves a home; and in order that they might live, he granted them the right to beg in the city on two days a week. The city, however, was not over-pleased to have them, and moves were made to have them rehoused further afield.

The "Dip" made a profound impression on Cheshire. It was shocking that human beings could be reduced to such a state of degradation, though this is not uncommon in India. But what struck him was the cleanliness and tidiness of everything, the care with which the lepers had made the most of what they had, the total absence of discontent, even though they longed for something more in keeping with human dignity. When Father Linus led him into the little open space in the middle of the colony that served as their communal hall, they ran into one of their huts, fetched out what were obviously their two best chairs—one would hardly have dared think they would support a man's weight—carefully polished them with a handkerchief, and ceremoniously invited their visitors to sit down. The one certain thing that emerged was that they did not want to leave the confines of Dehra Dun; nor, within the limits of medical safety, did they want to be segregated from their fellow-men. If possible, they wanted to stay in the vicinity of the "Dip," which they had come to know as their home, but in better buildings. Even Raphael, on the other side of the Rispana river, was too far and remote for them.

Cheshire decided to approach the municipality for some land for the lepers. He was told that there was certainly land available, for there was indeed plenty in the area, but the authorities would want a high wall to be built round the colony, and its members to be excluded from the town itself. He had a row at once about this proposed segregation, standing on the very plot of ground which he hoped he would get. In the end the long-drawn-out and tiring negotiations, involving many visits to many different departments, with the inevitable applications in triplicate, broke down.

Permission to take over the land across the river for Raphael had still not come through, although he couldn't help feeling that it would at any moment. And while this issue, so vital to all his future plans, still hung in the balance, he went off on his overdue tour of the Indian Homes and of Singapore. In Singapore he bought a second-hand ambulance for Raphael, in the hopeful expectation that it would fare better with the Indian Customs than the bus and the landrover had done.

In January, 1959, while Cheshire was still away, Lord and Lady Denning came to India to attend a legal conference, and they travelled up to Dehra Dun. There, at a small but moving ceremony on the top floor of the Cheshire Home at 16, Pritam Road—the crenellated Victorian palace where Margot, Sidney, Roy and Michael had camped out among the bees two years before—they inaugurated the concept of the International Home and training centre. Those who were present have not forgotten the eloquence and clarity of expression of Lord Denning in expounding an idea which was still very much in its infancy. From now on the idea carried the stamp of authority, and developments were to follow fast. A day or two later Cheshire arrived back from his tour, followed shortly after by Winifred Burton, the first matron of Staunton Harold, and Jane Wehner, a pathological laboratory technician from the Tropical Diseases Hospital, both of whom had volunteered to come to India to help to start Raphael. Then finally permission came through to use the land on the other side of the river.

That very day Cheshire went round to the municipality to ask if they would grant permission for a mains water supply to be carried across the river. Somehow he had a feeling that, behind the opposition to rehousing the lepers in the neighbourhood of the "Dip," there was a genuine desire to help him, if only they could find a means of doing so acceptable to all. The fact that the site for Raphael was outside the city limits, yet so close at hand, might prove the solution to the problem—if only the lepers themselves would change their minds and agree to go there. When permission for the water supply to be carried across the river suddenly came he was completely taken aback, since he was told that work could begin the next day. The truth was that he didn't have the money to pay for it, and had to stall, but not, thanks be to God, for very long.

At the end of the month, just about a year after he had moved in from Jamshedpur, Sue Ryder came for her first visit to India—in part to see the Indian Homes and something of the problems in the country, and in part to lay the foundations of Raphael. Together they went to the "Dip" and asked the lepers if they would come to them and identify their interests with theirs. After long consultation among themselves, noisy and even bellicose, the lepers said they would.

This first visit of Sue Ryder to Dehra Dun is very clear in my mind, since Cheshire has caught its highlights in a film which he made called *Share Thy Bread.* It is a moving record of Raphel. Sue's uninhibited and friendly greeting with folded hands of the first group of lepers she met set the seal on the new partnership between them.

The plan was to manage out of their own resources, such as they were, and to hope that money would come from somewhere. Mr. Nehru, during a brief holiday in the beautiful Kulu Valley in the Himalayan foothills, had sent a warm letter of encouragement and approval of the idea.

"All good things," he wrote, "have to start from small beginnings."

It was timely advice, for this was bigger than anything either of them had yet contemplated, and there was a temptation to start thinking in terms of big money. The planning was carried out on the top floor of Pritam Road, which had been set aside by the committee of the Dehra Dun Cheshire Home as a place apart for Cheshire and Sue Ryder. In return for this great kindness, he had repaired the roof of the house for them, and in the planning of his new enterprise, before Sue Ryder came out to join him, he had gone to endless lengths to keep down the cost. He would think twice before taking a bus to the city. I am ashamed to say that in all my years in India I have never ridden in a bus in a town, and I know that very few Englishmen or women have either.

Despite the continual and chronic lack of funds, once approval for taking over the land on the far side of the river had come through Sue and he went straight ahead with planning the move in. And here it is necessary to explain how yet another group of disabled human beings came to be incorporated in the new international unit. In the Cheshire Home itself in Pritam Road there were a number of children who were too mentally defective to fit into a Home where most of the patients were primarily physically disabled. It was decided, therefore, that Raphael would take over a number of these children, and so free beds for the more normal type of case. The move consequently had to take place in two separate but interconnected parts, and Raphael itself, from the outset, acquired the character of a settlement where different kinds of disability would come to be cared for, each in its own immediate environment, but within a community which would be under one administration and would grow up as one diverse but unified family to which other groups might well adhere as time went on. Thus the sometimes confusing agglomeration of disparate groups of people and disabilities in Raphael had its origin in an actual problem on the ground, a problem which could not be solved within the framework of the conventional type of Home, but might be tackled within a larger community.

Winifred Burton—"Barty"—and Jane Wehner had welcomed the idea of the mentally defective children, and they spent some time in familiarizing themselves with the problem, as well as preparing the site across the river. It was the dry season, the beautiful winter of northern India, so the river-bed was dry and relatively easy to cross. Cheshire had hired a large tent, the speciality of India, whose mills know better than those of any country how to make these spacious and comfortable canvas houses. This tent was put up in a little clearing near the bank, and was just big enough to hold eight children. A second tent was on the way from England, but had not arrived, so they appealed to John Martyn, the Headmaster of the Doon School, who came to the rescue by sending two of his senior boys across the river with two small tents, which they erected quickly and efficiently. Barty and Jane Wehner were to occupy one of them, while the other was set aside for an older woman patient who was more difficult to handle. The kitchen was in the open air, with an extraordinary makeshift cage for the larder and storeroom. The only item they had to buy was a roll of pig-wire with which to enclose the little camp.

The move of the lepers had to wait on the arrival of the second tent from England. This would in any event only be a temporary arrangement to house the first lepers to leave the "Dip," since a young couple who had recently finished their service with the R.A.F. in Singapore had offered to come to India to help in the building of Raphael. The man was a carpenter, and the plan was that they should be entrusted with the building of the leprosy colony, since the girl, too, was remarkably handy at anything she was given to do in the building line.

At last the day came when the children were to be moved. They were loaded into the ambulance—which had turned up from Singapore—and the cavalcade set off across the bumpy bed of the Rispana River, without breaking any of the springs of the ancient vehicle. The route up the cliff on the far side was steep and twisty, and it was no joke getting the children up. At least four had to be carried the whole way. One was blind and insisted on racing ahead with her arms outstretched, regardless of what lay in front of her—and then there was Paiman.

Paiman was picked up off the street and brought to Cheshire completely out of her mind. She could not straighten her legs, and she waddled about on her haunches rather like a duck. When she got upset, which was fairly frequently, nothing could keep her where she was. In the Cheshire Home in Pritam Road she had lived in what they called the olive garden—a little compound at the back of the house surrounded by an eight-foot-high wall on three sides, with a lower wall on the fourth side cutting the compound off from the courtyard of the Home itself. Time and again Paiman escaped from the olive garden and had to be chased down the road, where she would scream abuse at passers-by and demand money from whoever came near her. Barty and Jane set themselves to work out a means of tying her so that she could move within the range of the cord, but could not escape and hurt herself. The prospect of taking her to Raphael was a worrying one, with the steep Rispana cliff on one side and jungle on the other three. However, for the moment she was so taken with the novelty of her new surroundings that she manœuvred herself up the cliff alone and approached the children's tent singing.

When Cheshire himself entered the tent he was reminded of the early days at St. Teresa's on the Lizard Peninsula in Cornwall. He remembered particularly the occasion when the Methodist minister had come up to see him, obviously suspicious of his religious intentions. Before getting on his motor-bike, as he was leaving the derelict building, he had said:

"Who would have thought there could be such peace and happiness inside so unpromising an exterior?"

This was exactly how Cheshire felt as he went into the old *shamiana* among the sal trees on top of the steep bank of the dried-up river. Outside, it might have been any old tent in any old corner of India. But inside it might have been a ward of the finest children's hospital in England, so brightly and tidily had Barty and Jane arranged their simple fittings. This impression was more than sentimental or superficial, for the children never looked back from the day they moved into Raphael. Paiman was never put on her lead again, and she escaped only once, when she came back on her own after having travelled barely a hundred yards. Two years later she was standing upright, and weighed twice as much as when she had first arrived at the Home. She was to be put in charge of all the washing-up and of the storing of the plates and cutlery.

As that first evening came to a close, it was clear that the impossible had happened again; there was the little camp to prove it, and the pipeline which carried the water across the river in a trench twenty feet below its stony bed. Darkness had come while the children were eating their *chapattis* and curry from brand new bowls, sitting on their freshly filled mattresses. The *charpoys*—the string beds on which most people in India sleep—had been scrubbed and disinfected, so that the camp was like that of a Boy Scouts' troop at a jamboree. Cheshire lay in his ambulance on the river-bed, keeping guard; while in the camp above was the Gurkha night watchman, armed with a sharp *kukri* (knife), though in point of fact the poverty of the settlement was a much more effective protection than any Gurkha.

Cheshire's dream had been to settle down at Raphael and take charge personally of the settlement. From there he would keep in touch with developments in other parts of the world. In this feeling there had been a mixture of yearning to remain with the patients, and of desire to be released from his unending travels and the perpetual opening of garden fêtes. This role which he understandably wanted to be allowed to play was the very one which most of his friends and helpers would have given a lot for him to assume. It was the part of the romantic and withdrawn hero. But it was not to be. A much more complicated, yet prosaic, situation was to develop. Sue Ryder and Leonard Cheshire became engaged. Their personal lives and their two organizations had suddenly and unexpectedly become linked.

As April of 1959 approached and he was due to go down to Bombay to meet Sue for their marriage at the hands of Cardinal Gracias, the future looked uncertain, despite the happiness of the children in the little camp. News had come from Bombay that the tent from England had been cleared through the Customs, and was on its way up to Dehra Dun. The advance party of lepers was standing by; they were now longing to move in. But who was to look after them? And who, moreover, was to take administrative charge of the whole project? Jane and Barty were fully committed to looking after the children and could not be given any other responsibilities. Chippy and Stella, the ex-R.A.F. couple from Singapore, were due fairly soon, and they would be competent builders of the cottages Cheshire had planned; but beyond that they were unknown quantities. They could hardly be given charge of an embryonic leprosy colony in a country which neither of them knew. In any case, at this point Cheshire did not even know how they would fit in with the two girls who were running the children's Home. The latter and the lepers' colony would be fairly close to one another, and there would be inevitable problems of liaison and co-ordination. Sue and he had planned to go to Australia shortly after their wedding in the hope of raising support and money there, and after a brief return visit to India would be going on to England for the summer programme. Raphael would inevitably have to stand on its own feet and build itself up without either a local committee to take charge or the presence of Sue or himself on the spot to guide the infant project in its earliest stages of life.

Exactly five days before he had arranged to leave Dehra Dun for Poona to fulfil an undertaking to open a Home there, and at the same time to make a short Holy Week Retreat at the Jesuit Seminary, a letter arrived from a Bengali widow living in Jamshedpur. Her name was Ava Dhar. Her children had grown up and gone away, she had been an invalid for six years but was now better, and she was writing to him because they had met in Jamshedpur two years earlier, when she had asked him about the Foundation. She was wondering now whether he had any place into which she could fit and give whatever remained of her life. He sent a telegram there and then asking if she could come that very night to talk things over.

Ava Dhar left Jamshedpur, a thousand miles away, the next day. When Sue and Leonard got back to Dehra Dun on the 7th of April after their wedding in Bombay she was already installed as secretary, housekeeper and administrator of Raphael, a gift from Heaven indeed.

A touching wedding reception was given to them in the *shamiana* among the sal trees. The lepers and the children were there, Barty and Jane, Auntie Dot, of whom I shall write shortly, and Ava Dhar, also the Gurkha with his *kukri*. Leonard and Sue were garlanded, there was singing and the handing round of sweets. The joining of their two lives was the beginning of a new life for so many of these simple, friendly people who had now found a home in this beautiful place.

Sue's and Cheshire's marriage was clearly an event of the greatest significance for the work which each was doing. For Cheshire and his movement it had an importance which none of us appreciated at the time. In the first place, it was to ensure that success did not go to our heads and endanger the long-term prospects, for Sue Ryder was to reinforce Cheshire's insistence on self-denial and poverty. Secondly, they would be able to give strength to each other and to each other's supporters which was to mean added opportunities for the relief of suffering, opportunities which they both felt had been missed by each of them individually in the past. And incidentally, since their base was to be in England at Sue's beautiful sixteenth-century Suffolk house, which she used for the rehabilitation and resettlement of her charges—the survivors of the concentration camps—he was to find himself spending more of his time in England than would have been the case if he had not married.

I was to meet Ava Dhar not so very long after she installed herself at Dehra Dun, and to see for myself the remarkable strides that had been made within a few months. In January, 1960, I went to India for my firm and spent six weeks passing back and forth across the country, visiting factories and business-centres. In doing so I couldn't help calling in at the Cheshire Homes, of which there were now ten in India, and which were so situated that I could visit them all without doing violence to my business conscience. On the Sunday I was in Delhi I drove up to Dehra Dun, saw the Cheshire Home in Pritam Road and went to lunch with an old friend of my mother-in-law, Mrs. Rawlley, an Englishwoman who had married an Indian. Her husband had been a Government servant in the Punjab, and had retired to Dehra Dun. His wife, known to all as Auntie Dot, had met Cheshire, and had taken on the voluntary job of welfare officer for Raphael. In fact, she and Ava

Dhar were now providing the drive and the administration for this remarkable experiment. Over lunch in Auntie Dot's bungalow in the cantonment, I heard much of the story which has been described in the preceding pages, not only from my hostess but also from Ava Dhar and Barty, who were fellow-guests.

After lunch we drove across the dried-up river-bed to the thriving little settlement on the far bank. As we jolted across over the pebbles and the potholes, Barty told me how different the crossing was during the rainy season, when the river is in spate with the melted snow-waters from the Himalayas, which come roaring down in a torrent for three or four months. They had to choose moments when the current was less fierce, and battle across as best they could with stores and provisions, all of which had to come from the town three miles away. On one occasion she was cycling through on their old bicycle with a load of vegetables when she misjudged the current. She was swept off the saddle, but managed to hold on to the string bag with the vegetables, and swam and waded to the far bank.

"What happened to the bike?" I asked her.

"We got it back next day a mile downstrean. It was a bit bent, but otherwise all right."

We climbed up the steep sides of the bank in the large American car which I had borrowed from my brother-in-law in Delhi, and came to a halt on the flat among the sal trees. I parked the car beside the old ambulance from Singapore. The site certainly lived up to Cheshire's description. It was cut off from the city on the far side of the river, and was a place of peace and beauty as only the remote, untouched Indian countryside can be. Clustered round the ambulance to welcome us were about twenty lepers, hill people from this part of the country, cheerful and amusing despite their deformities. There were men and women and children. They gave us a warm welcome. With them were Chippy and Stella, who had already built four smart-looking huts made of wooden planks on cemented plinths, each hut divided into four parts, to house four families. The huts, about twenty yards apart in the light jungle, were connected by paths, and there was a plan for many more. The fifth hut was half-built. Ava Dhar explained to me that as soon as it was up another group of families would be able to come across from the "Dip" on the far side of the town. They were now quite reconciled to their new home, and those who had not yet been accommodated were envious of those who were already re-housed, and wished to come over as soon as they could.

Later I was to be put in charge of the finances of Raphael, but at this time I had no idea of how it was all financed, so I asked Ava Dhar, "How do you do for money?" The old question.

"We have to depend on Leonard and Sue, who keep us in funds both for the new buildings which are needed to house the lepers and the children and for our living expenses. We do get money here, of course, but obviously we must be careful not to take money away from the Homes in India, especially from the Home in Dehra Dun. The Chief Minister of the State visited us the other day and gave us a very generous donation."

When Mr. Nehru visited Raphael a year later he gave over a thousand pounds towards the work. One of the most generous and timely gifts was to come from the Oxford Famine Relief Fund.

It was a sizeable undertaking. For not only had the growing family of people in the settlement to be fed, which involved the employment of some staff, and so a minimum expenditure on wages, but the houses had to be paid for—that is, the cement and the timber and the cost of carting it all across the river-bed in bullock-carts from the city. Much of the labour costs was being saved by the skilled voluntary work of Chippy and Stella, but they were concentrating on the leper colony, which, of course, was now only part of the settlement. The mentally retarded children, who had moved in first, had been taken out of the tent by this time, and were housed in a really beautiful single-storey building constructed round a courtyard which had been designed by Cheshire and Sue Ryder, and had been built by Mr. Gupta, a contractor from the town who entered with praiseworthy understanding into the spirit of the enterprise and never pressed for the payment of his bills, so that work could go on even if the money was irregular in coming from England.

The children's Home was about a quarter of a mile from the leper colony, and separated from it by the light jungle which characterizes the place. It had been built on the northern extremity of the twenty-five acres which had been leased to Cheshire by the State Government, and it looked out from the edge of the jungle at the great barrier of the Himalayas, whose foothills rose sharply from Dehra Dun to five thousand feet, with the hill station of Mussourie, well-known in Anglo-Indian days and now the exiled home of the Dalai Lama, perched up on a ridge away to the north-west.

Barty and Jane Wehner showed me round the lovely Home, which had two dormitories along each side of the centre courtyard of lawn and flower-beds. There was a single bedroom at each end of the dormitories where they slept.

"A bit different from the little tent where we slept on our *charpoys* at the beginning, with our kitbags as bedside tables!" said Barty.

The children were playing in a large wired-in compound at the side of the Home, and there was no doubt that they were happy within the limitations of their mental state. I saw the famous Paiman, who bore little resemblance to the sad wreck of a child she must have been when she first came to the Cheshire Home in Pritam Road. I took a number of coloured photos, we had tea, and then the time came to leave for the hundred-and-fifty mile drive back to Delhi. After the usual and inevitable shaky start, this new experiment was clearly on the way to being a success, if only the necessary funds —nothing very spectacular—could be raised in England and elsewhere to keep it going, and to enable the imaginative ideas of Sue and Leonard Cheshire to be put into effect. The absence of a committee certainly ensured that the character and the purpose of the settlement would not be changed or deflected by the sort of influences which sooner or later seem to affect committees of Homes in every land once they are secure and successful; but it also meant that the founders had to have devoted and efficient volunteers to administer the project and to provide the care, understanding and kindness which this rather special type of work called for. Here these were all very much in evidence in the little team to which I waved goodbye as the shadows fell over the Himalayas.

All the same, I couldn't help wondering how long this small handful of devoted women, Indian and English, could maintain the necessary momentum to keep this growing community alive, let alone make it expand. They seemed so frail and so far from the stable, secure, efficient Cheshire Homes in England, with their well-paid staff, their well-equipped wards and kitchens, their loyal and numerous voluntary helpers. If only the Homes in England could learn about this gallant adventure and capture through their imagination something of its spirit and of its significance, I felt there might well be many volunteers to join that little group on the river bank which was fading from view in the swift Indian twilight.

The work progressed. Cheshire and Sue Ryder were able to send out money from time to time, so that more mouths could be fed and gradually more huts could be built to enable more of the lepers to come across from the "Dip." A school was built for the mentally backward children, and an Australian girl, Pamela Breslin, whom the Cheshires had met on their first visit there soon after their marriage, volunteered to come to India to teach the children.

When this degree of progress was reported to Mr. Nehru, in 1961, he told Cheshire that he would like to see Raphael for himself. His visit was fitted into a busy tour of the north of India; he had five public meetings on the same day as the visit to Raphael, one of them involving an eighty-minute speech. He was due to arrive shortly before dusk. There had not been enough money yet to carry electricity across the river to the settlement on the far bank, so this posed a problem from the start. Ava Dhar decided that they would use Divali lights placed along the paths where Mr. Nehru would go. Anyone who has been fortunate enough to experience Divali, the Festival of Lights, in India will recall the warm and gentle glow given out by the little clay saucers with their wicks floating in coconut oil, and the cheerful light which they spread from their myriad flickering lamps.

The Prime Minister arrived ninety minutes late, well after the sun had gone down over the Himalayas. He was first taken to the leper colony, where he stopped to speak to them and asked them many questions.

Later, after he had left the settlement to return to Dehra Dun, he visited the last seventy-five who were still left behind in the "Dip." He spent a long time with them, every now and then stopping as he walked through their homes of sacking and corrugated sheets to hand them a flower from the garlands with which he had been presented at Raphael.

But what moved him most visibly at Raphael was the children in the care of Pamela Breslin, for they were so happy, and so changed from the miserable state in which he knew only too well they must have been brought into Cheshire's care.

The fact that Sue Ryder, at this very moment, was following up her break through into Poland by reaching an agreement with Yugoslavia and Greece appealed immensely to Mr. Nehru, who appreciated that it was this element in particular which would put the work on a truly international basis. The lepers and the helpless children touched his heart; the proposition of a mission to relieve suffering in which both East and West, Communist and Capitalist, could have an equal part undoubtedly fired his imagination.

My wife was in India two months later, and she too visited Raphael and saw these children, who clearly loved the bright, attractive Australian girl who had come from so far away and from such a very different kind of environment to care for them and teach them the basic joys of community life. This sight moved her to tears.

Pamela Breslin was outstanding among the pioneers who volunteered from many different parts of the world to work at Raphael. She was working in Brisbane as a qualified teacher of the deaf and dumb when Cheshire and Sue Ryder were doing their whirlwind tour of Australia immediately after their marriage. She came to see them, offered her services, and was accepted on the spot. Although she was by no means well off, she managed in some extraordinary fashion to find her fare to India, and offered to work at Dehra Dun for two years. When she arrived at the end of her long and strange journey and saw the children she was to work with she very nearly gave up there and then, so awed was she at the prospect of trying to teach a class of thirty backward Indian children, the majority of whom could not utter a single articulate sound. But she set her mind to the task, and by her own unaided efforts she built up in two years what has become the show-piece of Raphael.

She was down to earth, extremely forthright, insistent on being obeyed and yet fond of the children to the point of tears on occasions. Her technique was to fit out an extremely attractive classroom with books, pictures and charts which the children could never hope to understand, but which somehow gave them the feeling that it was an important room. She taught them nursery rhymes by means of huge colourful pictures, by singing and by gesticulation; she got them to draw extraordinary patterns, first with coloured pencils and then with paints; she made them try to identify colours, which they never succeeded in doing; she taught them simple prayers, singing, gymnastics and ball-games. It was not very academic, but the effect on the children was striking in that it seemed to give them a sense of purpose and then an order and tranquillity in their strange little lives. They grew to love their school so much, in fact, that the worst punishment they could be given was to be told, "No school." Today the number of children has gone up to forty-five, housed in two permanent buildings—the one I saw early in 1960 has been duplicated—each costing £3,500.

At a gathering of people at Family Day at Alne Hall in Yorkshire the year after Nehru's visit, John Martyn, the Headmaster of the Doon School, described the occasion when Pamela Breslin left Raphael at the end of the two years which she had promised to Cheshire, and went to Singapore to get married. At this time he happened to have on the teaching staff of his school a young Englishman from the Voluntary Service Overseas. On Pamela Breslin's wedding-day they had both been invited by the Franciscan nuns who had taken her place with the children to come over to Raphael, as the children had arranged something special. The something special turned out to be an Indian wedding ceremony organized round a doll which they had dressed up as Pamela. All they needed to make the ceremony complete was the bridegroom. When the children saw the young Englishman they insisted that he should be married to the doll. And so these children, who had been outcast and unresponsive and in some cases even aggressive, had developed in a quite extraordinary way under the stimulus of devoted women such as Barty, Jane Wehner and Pamela Breslin.

Every month now I receive by airmail the detailed accounts of the Raphael settlement, beautifully typed and set out by Ava Dhar. Sometimes there are descriptions in her covering letters of highlights of the preceding month. The last one I received before writing this chapter contained a short and unadorned account of the kind of incident which has happened only too often in the monsoon months, and will happen again until we have been able to build some kind of bridge which will make it safe for landrovers at least to cross in these rainy months when the river is in spate:

"Father Gilbert described to us his misadventure while crossing the Rispana in his jeep on the evening of July 18th with another priest and four children. The vehicle landed in an unseen hole under the water and partially turned over, the water streaming in and nearly drowning the children. With the help of some of the leprosy patients who were watching from the bank, the car was pulled out and pushed through to safety.

"Servants, workmen and tradespeople risk their lives daily in this season to get across to accomplish their jobs. When the monthly rations for the various units are sent over it is a morning's operation. They are usually carried across the stream as far as possible in a bullock cart, and then handed over to the leprosy patients or the servants to carry up one by one. In view of these difficulties, I think we must try to have some kind of Irish causeway, especially if the hospital is to go up."

Like the children's Home, the leprosy colony has made big strides since the day early in April of 1959 when the first eight patients moved into the Army tent. Today there are just over a hundred, most of them married, the rest mainly single men. The married couples each have a room and a good-sized veranda on which their *chula*—the Indian cooking stove—is sited. The houses are different in size and shape, some being designed for four families, some for six. Each family does its own cooking, and rations are distributed once a week. This is a lengthy and meticulous operation, lasting practically the whole day, for every item has to be weighed and checked down to the last ounce of tea. The colony has its own *panchayat*, or village council, for the solution of internal disputes and to act as a channel between the patients and the administration of Raphael. Auntie Dot comes over several times a week from her house in the cantonment area beyond the river, and carries out the difficult job of welfare officer in charge of the colony. The doctor calls once a week, and a trained medical orderly gives injections, treats ulcers and does the dressings. Most of the leprosy families keep chickens, which provide them with a small source of revenue, and a communal poultry yard has been started up. This, with some weaving, which they have also started, brings in some income to the colony.

All this seems a far cry from the V.I.P. experiment of 1947 and 1948, yet one hears across the years a faint echo of those early ideas in this new experiment which is taking place so far away from the original one, and with such very different people; in between there has been such an accumulation of experience in the field of human suffering. In this leprosy colony one patient is a shoemaker, another a tailor, and between them all they manage to keep the colony tidy, and they do the clearing and shoring up of the river bank necessary for its expansion.

On the capital side a house costs £160 for a family, a four-family unit costing about £650 to build. Maintenance is £2 a month per head. There is a little school run quite informally for the children of the colony by one of the patients.

Sue Ryder's idea is to take from the colony the children

who are as yet uninfected, but who will in time inevitably contract the disease, and put them in a separate children's Home within the settlement, segregated from those parents who have leprosy, or are alcoholic, or for some other reason cannot look after their children. They will not be far away, but will be brought up and educated in happy and healthy surroundings. This school has now started, and is called "Sue's school." At first the parents were unwilling to give up their children, but gradually they are doing so, and in this way a further step forward has been taken.

With experience and funds, the Cheshires also hope to form at Raphael a small settlement within the larger one especially set aside for young and destitute children, who in turn can contribute their share to the happiness of patients and staff throughout the settlement and finally will go out into the new India equipped and trained to be useful citizens.

Cheshire and Sue Ryder have planned Raphael not as a Home, but as a village of Homes. Each Home will cater for a particular category or age-group of the chronic sick, so that every patient can live in the specialized environment that his particular disability requires, and in a unit which is small enough to give him the feeling of belonging to a family. The urge to belong somewhere, which seems to be felt as strongly by a completely uneducated and neglected child in India as by a wealthy orphan in the West, is apparent to all; but the creation of a truly family atmosphere within an institution is a very difficult matter. Creating this atmosphere for more than thirty or forty people is the aim of Raphael, where the hope is to build up to an overall number of six hundred or more, the family spirit being retained within the individual units. In addition, such a village of Homes would be able to absorb the urgent and difficult cases which Cheshire and his wife are increasingly coming to regard as a real problem, in view of the resistance which is becoming evident in the committee system, and in the conventional thirty-five-patient Homes all over the world, to the acceptance of heavy nursing cases.

Ava Dhar referred, in the letter I have just quoted, to a hospital. The plan on which a number of people are now working, under the impetus of Cheshire and Sue Ryder, is the building of a modern, well-equipped hospital in the centre of Raphael in which can be concentrated all the specialized surgical, medical and therapeutic facilities required by patients of this sort. This will mean that the individual Homes can be simply and cheaply built without the specialized facilities which they would otherwise have to have. In addition, since the hospital will carry its own doctor and trained medical staff, the Homes can be staffed by semi-trained people, rather more akin to house-mothers than qualified nurses. When a patient in one of the Homes becomes critically ill he would not be nursed in the Home itself, but would be removed into the hospital, a more practical and economic way of handling the problem, which would still make the patient feel that he belonged to one family. Furthermore, in this way Raphael would be able to give remedial and therapeutic treatment not only to its own patients, but to all the many in the Cheshire Homes scattered throughout India, who would otherwise have to go without this treatment, for the load on India's hospitals is so great that they can never hope to give treatment of this kind to chronic patients.

It is the Cheshires' belief, too, that by having so many patients of varying disabilities in the one settlement there should be a greater chance of making it self-supporting and of giving each patient a constructive part to play. Already, as we have seen, several of the leprosy patients at Raphael have taken up their former trades and are beginning in a small way to earn their living. Clearly, many will always be incapable of doing anything at all, but as Raphael will in time have its own laundry, shops, bakery, farm and vegetable gardens, brace-making shop and other departments, there should be a good chance that many of the patients will be absorbed into one or other of these productive activities.

I remembered the words of Frank Spath at Le Court, the disabled editor of *The Cheshire Smile*, when he had told me of the feelings and aspirations of the chronically ill, that they wished above all to feel they were wanted and that they were useful. Here at Raphael these sorely handicapped villagers from the foothills of the Himalayas were beginning to realize both these deep human needs on the bank of the Rispana River.

CHAPTER THIRTEEN

THE STONES OF SAN DAMIANO

"WHO WILL GIVE STONES for the rebuilding of San Damiano?"

Soon after Francesco Bernardone had broken with his father and had begun to visit the lepers at Gubbio, he passed close to the church of San Damiano. It stood on a hill in a grove of olive trees. It was a beautiful place, but the church itself had fallen into ruins. Francis stayed to pray, and for the second time he heard God speaking to him. It was the voice of a friend, who told him to repair His ruined church. Some time passed before the opportunity came to start the work. When it did come, many people from Assisi who had thought Francis mad to give up the life of a rich man's son carried stones and building material up the hill, and in due course the church was rebuilt. Francis had done most of the work, but many others had helped him.

When I began this book I read the life of St. Francis; and his story—particularly the episode of San Damiano—struck a chord. For, just as the rebuilding of a ruined church was a task which one man alone could never have accomplished, so the achievements of Leonard Cheshire, with which those of his remarkable wife have now been merged, would have been impossible without the help of others. That so much has in fact been done can perhaps be explained in terms of what happened in Assisi so long ago. There is a lesson here for all of us, the lesson that we must set about what each of us is able to do, what we can actually see needs to be done; and, although it has been said so often that it has become a cliché, it is indeed true that big things can come from small beginnings, that it is better to get on with something practical, however small, than to think up big plans for the future. The truth of this lesson lies in the answer it provides to the objection which is so often raised: "What can I do, an ordinary person, in the face of such a huge problem?" Ordinary people were so surprised that a young man and woman should have the nerve to tackle, single-handed and untrained, such a colossal task that they felt impelled to take off their coats and help. Having carried some of the stones to the top of the hill, they have been amazed at how comparatively easy the rest of it is if there is inspired leadership, teamwork and a minimum of red tape. The trouble in the Cheshire movement has been that, as the number of teams grew and more Homes came to be established, so a frame of mind developed not unlike—though in a different and less spiritual context—that shown by the "top people" of Assisi in 1219, when the Franciscan movement had grown in size from its early beginnings of poverty and dedication.

At Whitsun of that year the Franciscans, assembling from all over Italy, held their chapter at the Portiuncula outside the town. The man who drew them together had been on a long preaching tour, and he was very tired. He was also not a little depressed because there were members of the order who were beginning to question the rightness of the oath of poverty on which he had insisted from the beginning. When the Portiuncula came into view he was surprised to see beside it a large stone building. It was, he learned, a chapter house which the people of Assisi had built for the brotherhood so that, however bad the weather, their meetings could take place in comfort. Francis was seldom angry, but on this occasion he lost his temper and asked those members of the order who had been with him the longest to climb with him to the roof of the new building. There they began to tear the stones apart and hurl them down to the ground below.

The leading citizens, who had paid for the chapter house and planned to give it to him, lost no time in making clear to the monk and his tough companions that the building was theirs and not yet his. Francis replied:

"If this house is yours, I have no wish to touch it."

He climbed down from the roof and went into his beloved church, Santa Maria degli Angeli, to pray. He had not accepted the gift, and in order to save it the givers had been forced to take it back.

From the beginning Cheshire has been constantly striving to maintain the spirit of poverty, and as his movement spreads the task seems to become more difficult. In the early days the struggle was simple and straightforward: it was to establish a Home out of virtually nothing and with almost no support. The very fact of aiming at this target ensured that the enterprise would be imbued with a spirit of sacrifice and comradeship; that anyone who had any part in it at all, whether it was one of the patients on his death-bed or a voluntary helper come up for the afternoon, was forced to respond to the challenge and so give the best that was in him.

There is one person, Frances Jeram, who appeared at the beginning of this story and who must also appear at the end. It was she who pointed out to him, from her professional knowledge, that they could claim grants for the maintenance of the patients at Le Court. And when Le Court was opened it was her courage and ability, through two crucial years, which held the administration of the little body of homeless and disabled people together behind the brilliant and erratic leadership of Cheshire. Once, after he had gone to Cornwall and all was black, he had told her late at night during a flying week-end visit that he would hand the whole thing over to the National Health Service. She had absolutely refused to agree, although she was by then on the verge of a breakdown. In the morning he admitted that she was right, and they continued to struggle.

I think this woman, the first of many who would run the Homes as he wished them to be run, understood at the very start both his objectives and his methods.

"Le Court could not have been what it was if there had been any money," she told me when we met years later, "and the movement could not have got anywhere without Le Court."

Similarly, the mixture of age groups, disabilities and temperaments at Le Court would never have coalesced into a family without Cheshire's inspiration, which extended to a gift for nursing and especially for caring for the dying. For he would give up everything when a patient was on the threshold of death and sleep on the floor of the dying man's room, easing, with an effort of will-power and an emptying of himself, his passing from the world; and this giving of himself, Frances said, resulted in there being no sadness at Le Court when death came. It was always a great victory in which they all took part; and when it came, as it did quite often in those early days, there was no gloom among the rest, only a genuine and wonderful happiness.

As the movement has grown and the work has taken Cheshire all over the world, so, as we have seen, he has been inexorably drawn further and further away from the patients, and particularly from the task of caring for them himself, for which he has such an astonishing gift. Now that ill health has once more intervened, this time to confine him for a year to England—though mercifully not to bed—he is turning his thoughts more and more to the question of nursing the chronic sick and the disabled. The problem in the Homes is a serious one, since there seems to be a growing shortage of staff who will do the work because they have a vocation for it, and this means that increasing numbers of highly qualified and so expensive nurses are being employed, and the cost of running the Homes is rising. What Sue Ryder and Cheshire are after is first of all their own corps of people who will do this work because they want to give something to the chronic sick, and who will do it as a vocation; secondly, they want to train such dedicated people into a corps which will comprise not only nurses, but all those categories needed in the care of the chronic sick, from doctors to cleaners, a corps that will be open to people of all nations.

Cheshire and his wife are convinced that the chronic sick should not be treated as if they are just another type of patient, but that they constitute a field entirely on their own and need an entirely fresh approach, even a new and specialized form of training for those who are to look after them. More State Registered nurses than ever are being employed in the Homes, all of whom have undergone a highly specialized training directed towards treating and overcoming temporary illness or disability. When they are faced with the chronic sick there is little pure nursing, and no cure can be expected. Only the most dedicated can be expected to find the work inspiring.

Cheshire has always felt that the emphasis must be placed on caring for the individual by making the sort of mental effort he had been able to make among his earliest patients at Le Court, so that they may forget their disability in the way in which their lives are organized and their outlook on life is moulded—so that, in fact, they are helped to feel that they are needed and have a real contribution to make. If this view is right—and I am confident, from what I have seen, that it is—then surely a less professional kind of attention is required, so that the highly trained nurses who are doing the work today will be relieved in order to do the kind of work for which they have been trained. During his coming enforced retirement from active operations it is likely that Cheshire, with the help of Sue Ryder, will concentrate on building up at Raphael a corps of dedicated helpers around the group of women who have already done so much for the work; and this corps will be drawn on by the Homes in Britain and abroad, so that the cost of running the Homes will be reduced and a more constructive approach to the patients should become possible. Their plan is to attract into their nursing corps men and women who will be ready to learn a simpler technique of nursing the chronic sick, and also the more difficult psychological skills which this dedicated task demands; people who will be ready to work in the Homes and the Raphael settlements for longer or shorter periods and in any part of the world where they may be required, and who will accept no pay other than pocket money. This plan may seem absurdly ambitious, but sufficient numbers have already come forward on the present *ad hoc* basis to indicate that something more organized, yet still essentially spiritual, may be possible.

From the earliest beginnings Cheshire has regarded the growth of the Homes, not in terms of an exciting success story, as some of us have tended to see it, but as a struggle between organization—the body—which is fundamentally materialistic, and idealism—the soul—which is fundamentally spiritual. Organization demands security, if not actual prosperity; it likes to have its own way and be its own master; it has vested interests in the shape of business and social connections which must not be jeopardized and which may, in fact, be advanced.

The spirit has different attributes. It wants to help those in need at its own cost; it looks upon shortage of money neither as a hindrance nor as an excuse for not bringing the help that is needed; it mistrusts human means of support and looks upon Providence as its guardian and benefactor. Cheshire has always sought to be convinced that Providence wished him to follow the course that his inclination told him to pursue—as when he tried to keep away from the *News Chronicle* reporter who came down to Le Court when they were out of money and almost out of hope, and when he infuriated Frances Jeram by appearing to be deliberately uninterested in the visit to Le Court of the Carnegie Trustees.

But he was always sufficiently practical to appreciate that idealism, if left to itself without an organization through which to work, must sooner or later give way to excess and finally defeat its own ends. Ideally, the spirit will steadily transform and spiritualize the organization until finally there is no conflict, but only a harmonious and habitual doing of good. He recognized, too, that such is the state of human nature that this seldom, if ever, happens and the struggle continues until the end of time.

A fact which must also be taken into account is that the exciting success story has concealed at different times and in different places many weaknesses. The most dangerous, for the majority of us, has been our insistence on money first, which has dogged the footsteps of most Homes. It was the cry in the early days of the new St. Teresa's; also, in varying degrees, of most of those connected with St. Cecilia's. Today, when much seems to have been achieved, it is still more in evidence; very few committees think in terms of occupying a building without money in the bank. In England, once the informal partnership had been established between Cheshire and the local authorities which grew from those first claims put in at Le Court by Frances Jeram, county health authorities have made weekly maintenance grants to all the Homes for patients falling within their sphere of responsibility; and while these grants meet about two-thirds of the running expenses of the Homes there is always the one-third gap still left to fill, which has to be made good by private donations, fêtes and other fund-raising activities. Not many of the patients can afford to contribute to their own upkeep, and it has always surprised me how few patients seem to come from families with independent means. This is probably because those who can afford to stay at home or enter private nursing-homes are reluctant to abandon their independent way of life, whatever the hardships for themselves or their relations. And this does mean that the committees, especially of new Homes, tend to be obsessed with thoughts of money and expenditure, an obsession which some of the more meticulous local authorities do little to relieve.

It might be thought that this emphasis on financial security signifies that the idealism of the movement is weakening. This in fact is not the case. Each committee, in different ways, has had its eyes opened, and to a greater or lesser extent has come to see that money is not the first consideration. There have from time to time been harsh judgments in this story of the periodic lapses into materialism of management committees; yet as one looks back it is astonishing, and very heartening, to realize that many committees, some consciously and others without knowing it, have come to attach less importance to money and to show more willingness to act first and find the money afterwards; even, perhaps, to think in terms of helping other Homes. I myself lead a Jekyll and Hyde existence, taking part during the day in an organization which lends substantial sums of money on interest and against security in transactions which are clothed in elaborate and sometimes long-drawn-out legal documentation; and out of office hours find myself following the will-o'-the-wisp of Cheshire, handing out to bodies of people, whom I may never have met and occasionally have scarcely heard of, money which sometimes has not even come in at the time it is despatched. This ambivalence can be worrying, but at least it helps me to understand the difficulty committees experience in appreciating Cheshire's unusual methods.

Professor Cheshire himself used to say during the first

three years that money was the key to the whole thing. Then one day, when he was engaged in discussion as to who should be entrusted with the building of the new St. Teresa's, he remarked:

"Any fool can build a Home if he's got the money; what we want is someone who can do it without."

The committee of St. Teresa's soon overcame their early misgivings on this score when they discovered the response of the people of Cornwall, not only in money, but even more in voluntary work and personal sacrifice. Now St. Teresa's is in the van of much of the new development, especially in its friendly attitude to the Homes abroad—which is particularly encouraging, since one of Cheshire's most difficult tasks has been to make the Homes in Britain look out beyond themselves to the struggling Homes abroad.

This parochialism, which, however natural and inevitable, is nevertheless a serious weakness in the whole structure, has shown itself in many different forms. Le Court was in dismay at the prospect of a second Home; the Yorkshire Homes began by refusing to take in anyone from outside Yorkshire; all the English Homes, without exception, were unhappy at the prospect of Cheshire disappearing, as they imagined for ever, to India. In the autumn of 1955, when the little party of four was getting ready at Ampthill to set out on the journey to Bombay, Cheshire went down to Cornwall to attend a function at St. Teresa's. He had intended to weave into his talk something about the expedition. Jack Stephens said to him just before the speech: "For Heaven's sake don't talk to me about India. I've got quite enough on my hands with this lot without worrying about India." And now Jack, who in the winter of 1961-2 went on a strenuous trip to the Middle East, India and Ethiopia—it was the first time he had been east of Suez in his life—is the strongest advocate of the work abroad.

There are naturally other things, perhaps not so widespread, which nevertheless cause Cheshire concern. There is the tendency, now that the movement is more or less successful, for some people to come on to committees because they see it as the right thing to do. There is the common human weakness for power which men and women like Cheshire and Sue Ryder seem destined to expose wherever they see it. This particular trait manifests itself in ways that are sometimes not so obvious—for instance, in a sort of jealousy towards other incipient ventures not under the control of the Cheshire Foundation itself. The spirit of the take-over bid can be present in the world of charity, I think, just as it is in business.

The weak points in the fabric are not, of course, confined to those who have given up so much time, energy and money to this movement. As the Homes in Britain have become more solidly based and secure, some of the patients have become more demanding and self-centred, showing themselves to be as human as the rest of us. And this trend, which has begun to worry thoughtful people on the committees of several Homes, seems to have coincided with a weakening emphasis throughout the movement on religion. Partly from instinct, but more because of the advice which Cheshire received at the start of the movement from authoritative sources inside the Roman Catholic Church, he saw to it that the Homes were non-denominational. This did not mean that he was not passionately concerned that religion should be present in them, and that patients, helpers, staff and committees should be imbued with a spirit of sacrifice and dedication. This spirit, in his view, would be kept alive and renewed more readily and in the proper way if there were opportunities for worship within the Homes themselves.

I suppose it is inevitable, as Cheshire's personal influence is withdrawn, that emphasis on the spiritual aspect of the work should diminish. Here, as in other ways, the rapid advance has obscured some of the basic principles. Outside Britain, particularly in Asia, the position is different, for there the outward and visible signs of the Western creeds among which the work was born and grew up would be unacceptable to local sentiment and also to political feelings, and would contribute little to the work. This does not mean that the spirit of true religion is not present in those overseas Homes, for I have seen it myself, and in a most tangible way. In India and Africa and South-East Asia the many different races and communities, who find it difficult to co-operate in political and business life, meet and work together in friendship and unity of purpose in the Cheshire Homes.

It was the concept of a brotherhood transcending race and creed which brought Sue Ryder and Cheshire together in a common resolve to link their two undertakings. Although Sue's work has spread over a wide area and covers a multiplicity of activities, there has never been any real delegation of authority, for she has never lost personal contact with those for whom she has made herself responsible. She cooks and drives for them; visits all her hundred and fifty gaolbirds; chooses and wraps their Christmas presents; and, together with her devoted helpers at Cavendish and at Hickleton Hall in Yorkshire, is available always for all who want her. This, too, has its dangers, but it has meant that the spirit of the work has never wavered or been obscured; and it was this that appealed so greatly to the Poles and made possible what everyone thought was impossible. In a word, Cheshire and Sue Ryder each needed the other for their mutual strength and wellbeing, and together they have the opportunity of achieving what they could never have done alone—the building up of a world-wide family, a commonwealth of charitable institutions capable of working in harmony and unity for the greater good of those who suffer.

It has taken some little time, with doubts and differences of opinion, to see how this unity could be effected, but gradually the pattern has become clear. By a natural process of evolution the growing number of autonomous Cheshire Foundations, together with Sue Ryder's Forgotten Allies, which are themselves spreading into several countries, are now coalescing into a kind of commonwealth of like-minded people and institutions. They have called this embryonic coalition of independent bodies the Mission for the Relief of Suffering. It now has its constitution and rules. The list of founder members embraces fourteen autonomous institutions, starting with the Forgotten Allies Trust in England, Poland, Yugoslavia, Greece and Germany, and embracing the Cheshire Homes in India, Eire, Malaya, Nigeria, Jordan, Sierra Leone, Morocco and Hong Kong. Only the other day, in Market Mews, I ran into François de Vallembreuse, whom we met earlier in this story, when he accompanied Cheshire to Singapore. He has now identified himself with an organization in France which sends out dedicated people to countries as far apart as Korea and the Cameroons, where they work in the villages in the cause of rural development. Before going out to the underdeveloped countries, they undergo much the same kind of training at a settlement outside Paris as Cheshire has envisaged for his international workers at Raphael. François was immensely interested in the idea of the Mission for the Relief of Suffering, and it would not be surprising if the future holds some kind of association between the French body and the Mission. Even more striking is the request of the Polish Ministry of Health to be considered for membership; their warm reception of the idea of the Mission is to be discussed during this winter of 1962-3, when Sue Ryder goes back to Poland. And there is the fine leprosarium of Dr. Bandarawalla outside Poona in western India, which I have visited, and which has applied for membership.

The principal concern of Cheshire and Sue Ryder is that the Mission shall not become just a club for talking and for patting one another on the back, but that, irrespective of national boundaries, it shall become a really effective means of bringing greater relief to those in need; and the best model they can find, both as an illustration and as a guide, is the free association of nations which comprise the Commonwealth. They hope that a person of international standing acceptable to both East and West will become the head of this new association of like-minded institutions.

As we come to the present evolution of the Mission for the Relief of Suffering, two questions have to be answered. What is the message that Cheshire and Sue Ryder are trying to convey, and how long will their achievements last after they have gone?

To begin with, I suppose that they would not describe what they are trying to do by the high-sounding word "message." I believe they would say that in this twentieth century the relief of suffering, like so much else, has become increasingly the responsibility of governments and organizations, becoming in the process more and more impersonal. In fact, the laudable efforts and strivings of many devoted people to bring socialized medicine and care to every section of increasingly affluent societies has resulted, paradoxically, in many of those newly enfranchised classes discovering an unexpected urge to recapture the personal touch both in the giving and in the receiving of help. They would say, I think, that all they are trying to do, in company with many other charities, is to fumble their way towards bringing humanity and compassion and, perhaps, a sense of humour into the world of suffering and pain.

On the question of what happens when they are gone, I have only had the very briefest of talks with Cheshire, and he expressed the down-to-earth view one would expect—anything which does not move forward and grow must in the long run wither and die. He expects, as he has always done, that any idea which proves to be sound, if it is in the hands of the right people, will expand and grow. It was because he found by trial and error that his formula for Homes for the chronic sick was sound that he confidently left his tender plants to be cultivated by others. If they have succeeded in the past, then surely they will continue to do so in the future. The fact that Homes have started without his personal presence and inspiration in places as far apart as Nigeria and Sierra Leone on one side of the world and Hong Kong on the other might be taken as an indication for the future and as to how this second question should be answered. I always thought that the turning point of the movement in England in the early days was not the founding of St. Cecilia's, remarkable as that particular incident was, but the way in which Alne Hall and White Windows, the first two Homes in the north of England, started without reference either to Cheshire himself or to his Trustees.

I have written before about the influence of religion in his own life and the effect I think his faith must have had in taking him so fast and so far. Prayer, I think, is at the heart of his life; and the focal point of much of his thinking is the Holy Land, where he saw to it that early on in the overseas work there should be a Home for children at Bethlehem. This Home, through no fault of his, may sooner or later have to be closed in favour of the more ambitious institution which is already being built at Amman, the capital of Jordan. But the time will come when there may well be a different sort of home or retreat at Bethlehem, perhaps linked with the Raphael settlements at Dehra Dun and at Godalming in Surrey (where they have started a second village of Homes for disabled married couples and the heavy nursing cases), for Cheshire's mind is never far from the place where Christ was born and died. My first inkling of this plan came when he asked me if some money which had been given to him by a friend could be temporarily diverted from the destination he had planned in order to buy some land he had just been offered at Bethlehem. He has bought this land on top of a little hill above Bethlehem, and here he hopes to found what will in effect be a monastery for the disabled, where those who feel drawn to the contemplative and the religious life, but who are barred from it because of their state of health, may lead a life of true religion and contemplation. Of necessity it will have to be confined to one religious denomination, since the disabled people there will be leading a religious life; but it may be that this initiative may inspire others to work for the same end according to their beliefs and conscience. It is his hope that this place near Bethlehem will become not just a power-house of prayer for the whole Mission but a model of how the disabled can turn their disabilities into a means of doing good to others.

In a letter which Cheshire wrote to me just as I was finishing this book he said about this, his latest plan and the one which is clearly close to his heart, that the highest role that anyone can play—although it is not necessarily the right one for every individual—is the contemplative life:

"I mean this," he wrote, "in its true religious sense, not in the sense of its application to anyone who retires from society and meditates. The monk who retires from the world to enter the cloister for the rest of his life is not running away from the world, any more than was the bomber pilot who took off as darkness was falling to bomb the enemy in his base. The cloister is his battleground, where he is going to fight for the salvation and good of the world, and if ever there was a time when the world needed prayer it is now."

He sees this new Home as yet another member of the Mission existing in its own right, and giving, perhaps, in its own good time yet another glimpse of what the Mission could achieve by welding many small and individually autonomous units into a real force for the relief of suffering.

This book has been about a movement. In describing the movement the individual who created it has of necessity been so enmeshed in the activities he planned and inspired that it has not been possible to paint a picture of the man himself. I was glad, therefore, when I came by chance on a description in an American magazine of a recent visit to the Holy Land by an American journalist.

"I had planned," the author wrote, "to spend part of the night in the Shepherds' field, but I was arrested by the police as a suspicious character. I was taken off to the police station, where I was able to establish my identity. The inspector apologized and asked where I would like to spend the night, so I said, 'In Bethlehem.' He then took me to the Casa Nova, where he was well known, and where he was able to get me a bed.

"I was outside on the balcony when a pleasant, youngish-looking man tapped me on the shoulder and told me that dinner was ready. I followed him into the dining-room. There was a table laid for two. I recalled having seen him several mornings earlier. I had been kneeling at the Holy Sepulchre when I caught my first glimpse of him. I had immediately noticed something intensely devout and reverent about the manner in which he walked in the Church. It was obvious this was his first time in the Church, and it was equally obvious that he was very conscious of the fact that he was walking on holy ground.

"As we talked I noticed his quick perception, his charming manner, his beautiful hands and a certain humility and zeal which could not be concealed even at dinner. When I mentioned that I had seen the Holy

Shroud at Turin he became very interested. I told him about my arrest, which had interfered with my plans to spend the night in the Shepherds' field.

" 'You were lucky to be arrested,' my companion said. 'The friar out there told me the place is full of snakes.' "

Later on, when they had parted, the American correspondent discovered the identity of his dinner companion that night in Bethlehem.

I had almost finished the story when I met Cherry Morris again, with whom it began. She asked me if I had been able to form any view about the size of the problem of the chronic sick, at any rate in our own country. I had to confess that from the statistical point of view I was as much at sea as I had been at the start. But one thing had certainly become clear in my mind—the only way to tackle the question of disability is to bring about a change of attitude among the healthy towards the permanently handicapped.

I then asked her a question which must sometimes trouble those who believe so deeply in Cheshire's work: What happens when they are gone? Will that be the end, and will it all have been for nothing?

"How could that be?" she said. "For even if between them they have done nothing else, they will have given hope and love to those men, women and children in so many lands, who without them would have been condemned to death in life."

CHAPTER FOURTEEN

AFTERWORD—1968

EARLY IN 1963 a questionnaire was sent out from Market Mews to almoners and welfare officers throughout Britain. The object was to find an answer to the question that Cheshire and the Trustees had been asking themselves for some time: "How is the Foundation answering the appeals for help it is constantly receiving?"

Replies came back from more than fifty almoners and seventy welfare officers. All of them had candidates for Cheshire Homes, but the size of their problems varied widely. Two principal facts emerged. The first was that there were no fewer than nine hundred current and pending cases on their lists. The second was more nebulous, yet more important: the narrowness of the line of demarcation between Regional Hospital Boards and Local Authorities with regard to responsibilities for the physically handicapped and the chronic sick. The Hospital Boards are charged with the responsibility for the chronic sick, since they normally require nursing, often a great deal of it; it was because this could result in such people, often quite young, being put into geriatric wards that the Cheshire Homes, almost by accident, had found themselves answering a very real need. Put bluntly, a hospital is no place for the chronic sick, especially if they are young. The Regional Hospital Boards can contract with Cheshire Homes to take their cases; in practice they seldom do. The reason is probably that when the Cheshire Homes started there were so few of them, and regional hospitals simply did not know of their existence;

while local authorities (which had responsibility for the disabled), back in those early days, did not have such a thing as a Home either for the chronic sick or for the disabled. The Homes, in their turn, had begun to realize that heavy nursing was often beyond their own capacity, since staffing was becoming increasingly difficult.

The enquiry, therefore, showed us clearly that the need was, if anything, greater than ever, especially for the permanently disabled who at the same time were heavy nursing cases. As if to underline this discovery, during 1965 the Homes turned down no fewer than 876 applications—over 70 per cent of the number of residents in all the Homes in Great Britain and Ireland. There was evidence, too, that the number of applicants was increasing all the time, as young chronic sick moved from special institutions and paediatric wards into those dreaded geriatric backwaters of our regional hospitals.

What was the Cheshire Foundation to do about this?

It was clear, from the replies to the 1963 questionnaire and from the experience of many Homes in subsequent years, that the trend was towards heavier cases. Cheshire's approach to the problem was to draw up plans for a Cheshire Foundation Service Corps to produce staff of all kinds specially trained for work in the Homes.

The Nursing or General Service Corps, as it came to be known, was established through the co-operation of two of the Homes—Ardeen, the first Irish Home, and Le Court, the first English Home. Recruiting was originally carried out in Ireland, but a steady flow of recruits came from Britain as well. The main part of their training took place in new buildings which were put up by the Foundation at Le Court with money provided by the Wolfson Foundation. The project also included the training, in the additional expertise covered by the simple word "care", of cooks, catering experts, occupational therapists and secretaries.

Since part of the nursing training took place in Treloar

Hospital near Le Court, inevitably the Corps was going to lose some girls who would be attracted to a career in hospital nursing. This was unavoidable; but since the training also included practical experience in the Homes it was hoped that many more would be fired by the special needs of the disabled and decide to stay with the Cheshire General Service Corps.

The questionnaire had also shown up a second need—the importance of suitable accommodation for married couples, one of whom was disabled. Their difficulties were especially great if it was the man who was disabled, since this often crippled their earning power! Cheshire's approach to this problem was to encourage in any way he could the development of communities or flats for such people. This was not easy and took some time, largely because the idea involved not only the provision of specially designed living accommodation but also the availability of nursing facilities for the disabled partner when the able partner was at work. A joint scheme with the Greater London Council for building a block of flats with a nursing wing at Tulse Hill in South London was on the drawing board for many years, and eventually came to fruition despite upheavals and changes.

Meanwhile, one of the most energetic and dedicated people in the Cheshire family, Pamela Farrell, whom we first met in Chapter One, had already forged ahead in this field. With her committee in Sussex, and with the help of Mr. Kleinwort, an influential and colourful City character, who used regularly to cycle to his office, she built a cluster of bungalows for married couples with one disabled partner in the grounds of the Heatherley Home. Heatherley shares with the couples in the bungalows its facilities and its wide range of activities, as well, of course, as its experience of nursing and care for the disabled; so they are able to live their own lives independently, yet in the knowledge that help and care are always at hand.

In 1962 Cheshire and his wife had embarked on a

venture in Surrey, where they were given land and a number of derelict wooden huts in a beautiful woodland setting near Godalming. The project was called Raphael, since it came under the umbrella of the Mission for the Relief of Suffering, as did the community of disabled people at Dehra Dun in India. For several years they tried to run it on their own without a local committee, since they wanted to take in the heavy cases which the Homes were increasingly reluctant to accept. They also fitted out several of the huts to accommodate married couples, one of whom was disabled.

In point of fact the Godalming project was so similar in nature to the ordinary Homes that the result would have been confusion if it had continued to be run under the Mission for the Relief of Suffering. In India the situation was different because there Raphael was internationally financed and staffed, undertaking a very different kind of work which the local Home could not manage. So it was decided that a committee of local people in and about Godalming should take over the project there and run it as a normal Cheshire Home, although it would be unlike most of the Homes since part of it would consist of the group of married couples and heavy nursing cases. White Windows in the West Riding of Yorkshire was also pressing on with this new idea, which might well prove to be one of the most significant adaptations of the Cheshire concept.

Another development which could have turned out to be even more revolutionary in the field of disabled living was that of the Day Centre. I think the idea was first discussed at our Annual Summer Conference in 1967, when Dr. Ayler Lewis, first Chairman of Dolywern's Management Committee, one of the Homes in Wales, pointed out that the Foundation was spending in the region of £100,000 to house a hundred disabled people yet at the same time it was turning away nine hundred others. He suggested the idea of Day Centre Homes in large urban areas to which disabled people could be brought who were being looked after by their families at home, often in circumstances of difficulty and hardship; they could spend the day at a Cheshire Home, if any suitably placed Home should be ready to make the experiment, and then return to their families in the evening. Here again, as with the bungalows and flats for married couples, there would be a combination of normal family life with the availability of care and nursing. Holme Lodge, the Nottingham Home, was already working on this idea.

These schemes were canvassed at the 1967 Conference, which had as its main subject of discussion "Rehabilitation and the Role of the Foundation". Rehabilitation had increasingly attracted many of us in the Foundation, especially those who had been to some of the international conferences for the disabled which were increasingly being held in different countries, where the effects of scientific and mechanical gadgetry often appeared so breathtaking. Cheshire had never shied away from any mechanical appliance which would help in the relief of suffering—in fact, he had been among the first to use every device the engineers could provide to help him in his work. At the same time he refused to be led by gadgetry into the field of rehabilitation and so be diverted, as he saw it, from his true path, care of the chronic sick who could never be rehabilitated. His words at the winding up of this 1967 Conference showed this determination:

"Two points seem to me to stand out from our discussion. First, that the heavily disabled, those who will never be able to live at home despite all the services provided by statutory and voluntary bodies, are always going to present us with a challenge. Secondly, that there is a pressing need for consultation with other bodies.

"On the first point I recognize that the heavily disabled will always come last in the order of official priorities. The view of statutory organizations seems to be that the greater need is to rehabilitate those who can be sent out into the world again to lead normal lives. Of course, this Conference is not the place to decide the pros and cons of that question. It is important, though, that the Foundation, having set itself to tackle the problem of the hard-core of heavily disabled who have nowhere to go, should stick to its task, and not be diverted."

He recalled the Home for crippled children started at Amman in Jordan. As a result of pressures exerted by some members of the Committee this Home had been turned into a Rehabilitation Unit, since, it was argued, this was the greatest need. When this happened it somehow became difficult to manage, and was handed over by the Cheshire Trustees to the Ministry of Health of the Jordan Government.

Cheshire said at this Conference: "If we attempt to go into the field of pure rehabilitation we find ourselves on quite a different footing and lose some of our former spirit." By this he meant that pure rehabilitation is different in nature from our concept of a Home, and requires not only much more finance than we are likely to be able to raise but also highly specialized staff and management.

The second point he made was the pressing need for consultation with other bodies.

"I find it very easy to be locked up in one's own little circle; to think that the whole world is this little world of our Homes; more difficult to see oneself as just a very small part of a much bigger world."

As the years have passed there has been little tendency in our own small part of the much bigger whole to stand still, for not only has the number of Homes both in Britain and overseas grown remarkably, but there has been a ferment of ideas within the Foundation and in a number of the Homes in Britain, notably Le Court. This period of growth in bricks and mortar has been a time of great activity in ideas; some of this new thinking has revolved round the part that residents should play in running their own lives. Should they, for instance, be represented on the Management Committee?

As in so much else, so in this controversial matter also Le Court took the lead. They made the experiment of having on the Management Committee not only representatives of the residents but also members of the staff; and while they were carrying out this experiment the whole problem was being looked at from another angle by one of the Trustees. Dr. Margaret Agerholm broke down the problem by classifying the disabled into two main groups: by degree of disability as assessed by independence, and by type of disablement.

Her two basic essentials for successful "capacity living" were, first, the stream-lining of daily living and of all "care" activities, so that these take up the minimum of time and effort; and, secondly, a social background as private and as flexible as possible in order to ensure the maximum individual choice of activity, and its distribution during the day.

In stream-lining daily living she listed only a few of the many devices which already exist, and which are being added to almost daily by the inventors of equipment, such as the Egerton and Campbell beds, electric hoists, patient-operated electronic controls for a wide variety of actions which can give an astonishing degree of independence to the most severely disabled, electric toilets, and many other devices. She pointed out that stream-lining can also be applied to individual activities such as feeding, writing and reading. I myself have come in touch with the talking book which carries tapes of a full-length novel in a cassette the size of a Penguin volume; although it was designed for the blind it has immense potential for the disabled once a broadly based library can be built up. Margaret Agerholm told us she was convinced that the possibilities of these devices in contributing to "capacity living", earning power and education had not yet been fully exploited.

Coming to the background against which disabled people can best carry on their lives, she considered that the severely disabled needed primarily two conditions, security and care, both of which are provided by the Cheshire Homes. But in accepting these the disabled only too often felt they were giving up two other conditions which they also value highly—privacy, and integration with the able-bodied community.

"I am well aware," she said, "that there are good, practical—and usually financial—reasons for the loss of privacy. The need for it, the need to get away from the crowd sometimes, not to eat every meal in company, to read, write, paint, etc., without interruption is a recurring theme when the disabled discuss their own views on institutional care."

In the context of integration with the able-bodied community she stated her own belief that the able-bodied need their disabled fellows as much as they themselves are needed by the disabled. She pointed to the experiment carried out in Copenhagen, where a special block of single-unit and family flats had been built, designed for disabled and for able-bodied people in the proportion of one disabled to two able-bodied tenants. Both the able and all the disabled who can do so go out to work as from any other block of flats, but in addition there are special facilities for those who require communal social life, room service, canteens and personal attendance. In this way security, care, privacy and integration with the community are obtained for the disabled, while the lonely, taking single-room accommodation, are soon drawn into the community by its social activities.

The flats which the Foundation built with the G.L.C. duly came to fruition, while the development of the bungalows for married couples pioneered by Heatherley was carried on by other Homes and eventually led to the

Foundation setting up a Housing Association. Meanwhile the other approach, possibly its necessary counterpart—participation in management—was proceeding at Le Court. In January 1968 the Le Court Management Committee produced its report on the two-year experiment in shared responsibility for management which it had carried out with the approval of the Trustees.

It began by setting out the consequences which had flowed from the haphazard giving of information to residents in the past—distrust between the residents and the Management Committee of one another's motives, distrust between residents and staff, and lack of interest by the staff in the problems to be overcome. It says much for the staff at Le Court that they considered the experiment to have been successful. With two exceptions, the Management Committee felt there was increased understanding and less suspicion among the residents of the Committee's motives when they had to make controversial decisions; consequently in difficult times there was less tension. The majority part of their contribution to the report ended thus:

"In a sentence, there has been a pronounced move from disunity towards wholeness, although there is still a long way to go."

There was, of course, a minority view which took the line accepted by all of us up till then, that administrative decisions are best taken by a small committee which stands apart from both residents and staff. This view was held then by the residents and committees at most of the Homes.

I suppose it is because Le Court has been established now for thirty-one years that it has become the pioneer in a number of aspects of Cheshire's work. The interesting thing, I think, is that in at least one Home these ideas are being developed, and that throughout the whole Cheshire family increasing attention is being given not just to the provision of care and shelter for the disabled, but to the finding of ways and means to help them live to capacity—in a word, to integrate with the able-bodied, whose need of them is probably greater than many able-bodied people would imagine or concede.

There is no doubt that the committees of many of the Homes learned with misgiving of the Le Court experiment; and to the extent that they were trying to carry out Cheshire's continuing aim of caring for the heavily disabled these misgivings were not only understandable but were felt also by Cheshire himself. Few heavily disabled men or women, requiring, as most of them do, regular nursing and attendance, have the desire or the capacity for the sustained and concentrated attention which administration and decision-making demands. The problem at Le Court has been that there are exceptions even among the heavily disabled, in the sense that some of them not only wish for responsibility but are capable of taking it. As against this it has to be admitted that the residents in most Homes argue that they do not want one of their own members to be in the privileged position of sitting on the Management Committee and having access to confidential information. As is often the case, the problem is one of method. Good communications are vital, and so is the right spirit. It must be acknowledged that Le Court's attempts to link this spirit with the right sort of administrative machinery require a high degree of sophisticated understanding between management, staff and residents.

If, then, the needs of the disabled in Britain were becoming more complex, what was the position overseas where the growth rate of Cheshire Homes had also been spectacular?

Two new factors were beginning to be discernible. For the first time Cheshire Homes were being started in non-English speaking countries; secondly, some of the Homes became embroiled in war.

The first of the Homes in non-English speaking

countries was the one in Lisbon. This was shortly followed by Homes in Morocco—in Tangier and Marrakesh. Two retired Englishmen, Alan Moysey-Adams, Chairman of Greathouse in Wiltshire, and Colonel Nigel Watson, went to Spain, South America and the Caribbean; as a result a Home was started in Santiago, capital of Chile, and preparatory work was done in Brazil and Argentina. In the Caribbean, which is, of course, for the most part English speaking, a wonderful Home was established in San Fernando, the large oil town in the south of Trinidad. Here a Trinidadian surgeon, Harry Collymore, an expert in the field of disability and rehabilitation who had never met Cheshire or seen a Cheshire Home, was able to create within the unpromising walls of the San Fernando Government Hospital a small Home which captured instantly the true Cheshire spirit.

Inevitably, as they grew, the Homes became involved in politics and, sadly, in war. Nigeria, one of the first countries to accept the Cheshire idea, had at the start no fewer than four Homes—in Lagos, Enugu, Ibadan and Port Harcourt. Of these two, Port Harcourt and Enugu, were lost in the fighting, but they were re-built after the war and now are flourishing. A new Home was started, at Orlu, during the war.

A brief description of the fate of the children's Home at Port Harcourt shows the kind of thing the Homes had to suffer if they were caught up in war.

In 1965 a pathetically small room with a kitchen attached was rented by the Port Harcourt Steering Committee, which consisted of Nigerians and expatriates, mainly British. Ted Newland of Shell was the Honorary Treasurer. A handful of disabled Nigerian children was soon living in the Home; at the same time the committee was vigorously raising funds to build a new Home in a better part of the town. Their target was £5,000. Ted Newland was posted away before the full amount had been collected, and his place was taken by another Shell man, Hedley Scott. The target was reached, and the new building was finished in 1967. It was opened by Cheshire in that year.

But more wonderful even than raising this money—a large sum for those days—and building a new Home was the arrival on the scene of a remarkable Ibo woman, Josephine Okali. Her husband had been killed in a road accident. One day Bishop Ofonya of Port Harcourt said to her: "Josephine, I have somebody and something who wants you." The somebody was Cheshire, the something the new Home with its initial complement of eleven children.

I met Helen Scott in London in July 1968. She told me what a superb person Josephine is. The new Obioma Home grew up around her. Oxfam, the big ex-patriate companies and many Nigerians helped with voluntary work, free paint, gifts of furniture and bedding in the traditional Cheshire fashion. They got a garden going so as to have their own vegetables. The plan was to house thirty children.

Then, in July 1967, the civil war came. On the 19th February, 1968, at 11.30 a.m., two bombers and two fighters of the Federal Air Force appeared over Port Harcourt. They dropped several bombs on the city, one of which hit the new Home. The Bishop, writing to Cheshire, said: "Thanks be to God, none of the poor orphans was killed by the bomb because they were all out at the time, including their Matron, Mrs. Josephine Okali herself."

The beautiful new Home at Enugu had also been destroyed, along with the rest of the capital of Biafra. Josephine, I was told by Helen Scott, had set out immediately after the bombing of Port Harcourt to see if she could reach Enugu, then still in Biafran hands, in order to bring the children from that Home down to Port Harcourt. She reached Orlu, half way to Enugu and ninety miles from Port Harcourt, then disappeared into the fog of war. After Port Harcourt had been taken by the Federal troops Hedley Scott returned to the town, but their party was not allowed into the district where the Obioma Home had been built. The team reported that Enugu was a ghost town.

Cheshire wrote to Josephine on 1st May, 1968, not knowing whether she was still alive. He said:

"Only this week we have completed the film on our West African Homes, which ends, as you will probably remember, with you and the children singing 'Good-bye'. That little sequence is the most moving in the whole film, and will leave a lasting impression in the minds of all who see it. You have set an example to all of us, and you may be sure that every Home we have here and abroad will be told the story of how you saved the children."

Josephine then emerged unscathed on the other side of the turmoil. Today she is Matron of the Home that was started at Orlu, where she had last been heard of after setting out on her epic journey.

On 9th April, 1969, Cheshire reported to his Trustees on a secret flight he had made into Biafra at the request of the Foreign Office. It was one of several such missions during the war, night flights which in some respects were as hazardous as those many others he had made from bases in Lincolnshire nearly thirty years before:

"One flies in on one of the relief planes from San Thomé to Uli airstrip sitting on bags of flour. Our own aircraft was a DC-6 flown by an ex-RAF Lancaster pilot from Lancashire with a German second pilot and a Belgian engineer. At Uli the landing lights are switched on some twenty seconds before touchdown and off long before the aircraft has come to a halt. I was driven fifty miles to Umuahia, the capital of Biafra, where I was given a bed by the Holy Ghost Fathers."

He succeeded in finding the remnants of the committees of the two Homes that had been destroyed and, amazingly, all the children, whom he reported safe and sound except for one who had died of an illness in hospital. He had found Josephine and the Matron of the Enugu Home. One of the most moving happenings of a movement which has not been short of them must have been the starting of a new Home for these waifs of civil war in the small enclave of a besieged Biafra into which the Founder had flown in a blacked-out aircraft bringing food and medicines, and at which he himself was able to be present.

"I was greeted in a remote village in the bush by eighteen people, the committee; it was headed by the local chief who placed the village hall at our disposal. A speech of welcome was made and the problems of setting up a new Home were discussed. It was a moving experience indeed to hear how the children had been evacuated under the noses of the oncoming troops."

It was at this time that Leonard Cheshire came near to bringing about a meeting between Ojukwu and Harold Wilson in Lagos which might well have opened the way to a ceasefire.

Another Home which suddenly found itself in the firing line was also a children's Home, in Bethlehem. Until the Arab-Israel war of June, 1967, it had been in Jordan territory and the committee was in Amman. The Matron did not live in the Home, and she only visited it during the day. Fadwa, a young Arab teacher of nineteen, lived in the Home, and when the war broke out she and the cook stayed with the children.

As soon as he heard of the outbreak of war Cheshire asked May Cutler, one of the most devoted and experienced of the small band of women who have pioneered so many of the overseas Homes, if she could fly to Bethlehem to take over. May was on holiday in England from her latest assignment abroad. She received Cheshire's telegram on the 12th June and was in Tel Aviv on the 14th.

She managed to reach Jerusalem the next day, where a friend of Sue Ryder, Mrs. Kahn, was able to get a permit from the Army Commander for both of them to visit the Home, now, of course, within the new frontier of Israel.

May Cutler and Mrs. Kahn found several children in the Home and very little food. Some of the children could walk, the rest were in wheel-chairs. The teacher and the cook were there to meet her; they had been with the children all the time.

The Management Committee was cut off from the Home: it was now on the other side of the new frontier beyond the Jordan. There was no money coming from there or from London, for there was no inward post either. Long afterwards, when May Cutler told me of her experience, she said:

"The little grocer's shop which was just down the road was very good to us, even when we had no money to pay at the end of the month. The father and son who ran it let us have anything we wanted, and the son was always willing to come and do odd jobs for us which we could not do ourselves. They were so very kind to us in all ways."

Just when things looked blackest, money from the Foundation in London reached the Home, a new committee was formed, and gifts of food, clothing and toys began to flow in again.

May Cutler left Bethlehem in February, 1968, by which time there were seventeen children. When I visited the Home in 1970 the airy house was full of happy and active children, humming with occupations and gaiety. An odd coincidence, I always thought afterwards, that its telephone number was Bethlehem 617, the number of probably the most famous squadron in the history of the Royal Air Force, that of the Dambusters, which Cheshire commanded during the last two years of the war.

The importance which Cheshire attaches to the work overseas was underlined by the decision to hold an International Conference in London during the summer of 1969. That year saw the twenty-first anniversary of the founding of Le Court. For a number of years Cheshire's aim, in Britain as well as overseas, had been to create an organization which would be able to carry on the work when he and his wife were gone. This had probably been achieved in the United Kingdom by that time. Abroad, conditions were naturally different, and I was always astounded how remarkably his spirit and ideas had been so readily transplanted and had taken root in the most unlikely places, where everything had seemed to conspire against them. In fact, it is no exaggeration to say that the spirit of achievement in a framework of poverty, ignorance and sometimes hostility is often more evident abroad than it is at home.

At that 1969 conference, at which there were delegates from Homes in Africa, India, Malaysia, Australia, South America, the Caribbean, Europe and the Mediterranean, an international council was established with five members from the overseas countries and two from Britain of which Cheshire was one. This new body asked the Trustees of the United Kingdom Foundation if they could set up in London on their behalf a small secretariat which would act for them as the international office of the overseas Foundations, and forge permanent links between all the Homes in the many countries where they had sprung up in such profusion and with such enthusiasm.

And it was at this point that I retired from the City of London, and from the family I had seen grow up so fast during the past fifteen years.

CHAPTER FIFTEEN

RIP VAN WINKLE

OCTOBER 1979. Ten years almost to the day since I had said a double goodbye, to Market Mews and to the City of London. In retirement on the north coast of Cornwall I had spoken once to the local branch of the W.I. about the Homes, I had been once to Saint Theresa's on Mounts Bay and had once seen Cheshire on TV. And now for a splendid three days I found myself back in the family for the 1979 annual conference and the special committee and Trustee meetings connected with it. In three days packed with reunions I met more old friends and, I think, made more new ones than would have been possible in months of travel, both in these islands and abroad.

The French have the phrase for it, although they rarely use it—the more things change the more they are the same. There was change all right. In 1956 Leonard Cheshire had stopped to chat with Earl Howe, washing his old Bentley in the Mews, and as a result—with the help of the National and Westminster Bank—we had bought the lease of one of his Mews cottages, Number Seven; now, twenty-three years later, the Trust also owned its two neighbours. One houses the overseas office, the other provides a home for the founder when he is in London, and for the many people who come to London from all over Britain and the world.

In that year of 1956, when I had taken over as Honorary Treasurer from Sir Archibald Jamieson, there were five Homes, six Trustees and £300 in the Bank. An Appeal in *The Times* had produced £9-2-0. At the 1979 conference Peter Rowley, who had taken over as Honorary Treasurer from Reg Emmett, the great guardian of our growth in the intervening years, mentioned almost casually that the fixed assets in the Balance Sheet stood at £7½ million and the properties were valued for insurance at £24 million; donations and legacies in 1978 had been just over £2 million. The capital of the Foundation was only 1·6 times the amount spent during the year on the two thousand residents, so that the money donated by a generous public was being spent on the work and was not being hoarded. I heard with astonishment that the 104 Homes of 1969 were now 179, of which more than a hundred were overseas; and that there are never fewer than three new Homes in the planning stage in Britain.

But there have been other more important changes from the era I knew, changes more significant than any figures. What are they?

A few months before I left, in the early seventies, the Trustees had already begun to question their own professionalism in the face of rising standards of care, technology and, most important of all, expectancy on the part of residents and public opinion. The old standards of the derelict stately home with a dozen beds in the ducal drawing room were not good enough any more. The searching of conscience had begun even ten years ago, and so we had set up a New Homes Committee of Trustees. I had chaired the first few meetings. Then it was taken on by Hampden Inskip, the Keith Joseph of the Foundation and an eminent Q.C., whose work for Le Court and the Nursing Corps has already found honourable mention in this story. During the period of this committee's existence the great surge forward had taken place from what Air Chief Marshal Sir Christopher Foxley-Norris, G.C.B., D.S.O., the present Chairman of the British Foundation, described in his conference address as "the small family business to the thriving and developing Foundation we are today". When he retired from the R.A.F. Sir Christopher Foxley-Norris offered Cheshire four days a week of his time to be Chairman of the Foundation rather than accept any of the full-time paid jobs he was offered. Peter Allott, engineer-businessman from the West Riding, is now Chairman of this key committee, which has been re-named the Homes Planning Committee. It has been at the heart of this astounding development. He gave me two hours the morning before the conference to tell me just what had happened.

"Since you were here the most important change," he began, "has been in the attitude of Government and of local authorities. As luck would have it, the last Government's Job Creation Scheme, as they called it, was heaven-sent for us. All we had to do was to get the Homes to put forward schemes of improvement which had to be 'socially desirable'—not difficult for us—and we could get cash grants from the Government. We must have benefited by over £250,000 from it; and this coincided with a time when the Foundation itself found increasing funds flowing in from donations and legacies. As a result we were able to be more generous with interest-free loans to the Homes than in your day. It was certainly the great leap forward for us." I asked him whether the Homes had come forward with a lot of new plans. "Some did and some were rather slow; and of course we can't dictate to Homes, as you very well know. Their independence, autonomy, if you like, under the umbrella of the Trust is a basic principle which obviously has to be respected, and in some cases we had to jolly them along by persuasion, you know how it is, and it worked."

I asked him what kind of changes had happened in the Homes since I left.

"Well, it's really a question of reacting to new pressures, pressures of public opinion and of the residents themselves. Few want to be in a ward any more. Most want single rooms, except the married couples, of course, and there are plenty of them."

"What other changes?"

"Well, I suppose the domiciliary care, or Home Support schemes, as we call them now." I asked him to explain. "We send staff out from a Home to disabled people who don't leave their own home so that during the day, when their own family may be out at work, our people wash and dress them, take them to the shops, perhaps, and generally care for them, so saving their families this extra work. The Counselling Service—you know about that, I suppose—well, this service is available to them as well."

I remembered about the Counselling Service. It had been started just before I left. Now it is well established and works under the general supervision of Henry Marking, one of the pioneer Trustees and Vice-Chairman of the Foundation. He was Managing Director of British Airways and is now Chairman of the British Tourist Authority. Without undermining the relationship between residents and staff in the Homes, these experienced Counsellors, two women and one man responsible to the Trust, living in the field and highly mobile, are there to give counsel, sympathy and support to residents, staff and management on the many problems they have; for the residents it is not just the difficulties they may experience in the Homes but outside matters as well, such as relations with their families—not by any means a simple business—financial problems, moral and intellectual difficulties; and like the confessional it is all in confidence.

Before he turned to prepare a paper for the meeting of the Trustees' Executive Committee, Peter told me something of the remarkable growth of the concept of individual houses, separate from a Cheshire Home yet built sufficiently close to enable the occupants, perhaps a married couple of whom one is disabled, to look to the

Home near by for medical and moral support, if they feel the need. The Grange Cheshire Home at Poole in Dorset has followed here in the footsteps of Pam Farrell at Heatherley. Under the stimulus of a committee member, Dr. James Burn, a Cheshire Home of only ten residents has been built on two and a half acres of land belonging to the Home, and a number of different sized bungalows are being sited on this land for occupation by disabled couples. And what is more the scheme is being financed by a new and quite separate Cheshire Housing Association, itself a recent innovation, which is being run by another old colleague on the Trust, Ben Worthington, Chairman of the Home at Matfen Hall in Northumberland and creator of the Home in County Durham, Murray House. I sat next to him during the conference and he told me that this Association can even qualify for grants from local authorities.

Before letting Peter Allott go I asked him what he considered to be the most important achievement of his Homes Planning Committee aside from the financial gains and the results in bricks and mortar which all could see.

"Without any doubt the increased respect felt by the Homes for the Trustees," he said firmly. "We have got to know the Homes much better now, and we meet the pioneering people who form Steering Committees to start up new Homes from the word Go; as a result the chaps in the field at last are beginning to realize that we know what we are talking about."

And this made me think of the French expression with which I started this chapter—"*plus ça change plus c'est la même chose*". One thing, it seemed to me, that hadn't changed since the days of the small family business was the people in it like Peter Allott, Hampden Inskip, Henry Marking and the rest, both the Trustees and the men and women in the field running the Homes. The spirit of voluntary service given so unstintingly, ferociously, almost, by expert men and women living busy lives in a competitive and inflationary world—this had not changed; and so long as such people can be found for the work nothing can stop its growth—or so it seemed to me. The value of the time given by so many gifted people to the Trust and to the Homes represents invisible income on the revenue side of the accounts which over the years must amount to hundreds of thousands of pounds.

And talking of revenue, a word must be said about the so-called capitation fees, the weekly grants which have always been made to Homes by local authorities ever since the early days at Le Court. Without them the Homes could scarcely have survived, for just as Cheshire, by providing a Home, beds, equipment and free management, has spared the local authorities this obligation, so they in turn have made grants for the upkeep of residents whom they would otherwise have had to care for themselves. During the pioneer and "small business" eras there had been constant arguments between local authorities and the Homes about the actual amounts, which, however high, could never be enough to meet the full running costs. Now, it seems, in the smoother waters into which the Cheshire vessel has sailed, these arguments are a thing of the past, probably because the local authorities have appreciated at long last that not only are the costs of the voluntary system so much less than those of the State but that their own costs, automatically swollen by an 8 per cent management fee, are to that extent pushed even higher above the Cheshire costs, where management, which is both personal and efficient, is free. How many millions must this not save the state? The opening speaker at the 1979 Conference was that warm and personal politician, now happily Minister for the Disabled, Reg Prentice. For me the most striking remark he made was that "the voluntary sector can never be bettered by local authorities. Your Foundation has made a contribution which the public sector could never have achieved."

And finally, in the sphere of administration it has been left to a firm of consultants, brought in recently by the Trustees in their search for new and better methods to professionalize their amateur approach, to point out that this enormous business is being administered from a head office which has the same number of people in it today as it did ten years ago, when there were fewer than half the number of Homes. Christopher Foxley-Norris, in his address to the Conference, said, "I am constantly greeted with surprise amounting to incredulity when I tell enquirers that our central staff amounts to thirteen salaried people, of whom five are part-time." So now that minuscule staff is to be increased to fifteen full-time and three part-time. There will be a Mental Care Officer, a Head of Counselling and Training and a Homes Planning Officer; and most probably in 1989, when the Homes may, perhaps, have passed the three hundred mark, now that America has realized the effectiveness of Leonard Cheshire's formula and is adapting it to its own life-style, there will probably still be only fifteen full-time and three part-time staff in the head office.

A feature of the work which started back in the dark ages, in Pitts Head Mews, now buried beneath the foundations of the Hilton Hotel, is care for the mentally handicapped; and in those days, a quarter of a century ago, that meant primarily children. Later, during the "small business" era, under the stimulus of Barry Richards, the Foundation set up "half-way houses" where men and women discharged from mental hospitals could adjust to work and life in the outside world. The Homes at Wimbledon were pioneering efforts in this field. During the last ten years growth in this complex and difficult area has suddenly become faster than in the field of the physically handicapped; and one of the most significant aspects today is provision for the mentally handicapped adolescent, who as a child has been cared for in Homes like Hawthorn Lodge in Dorchester and the Green at Christleton near Chester. In Farnham, for instance, a group of parents with mentally handicapped children has got together with the Foundation to build a Home for teenagers with funds supplied by the Area Health Authority, assisted by the Cheshire Housing Association, which will be able to draw on the advice of the Foundation and use, for example, the Counselling Service. A similar project is in preparation in Dorking. A successful example of such a Home already working in the Foundation is Fairfield House, Lyme Regis, which was started with money raised in a spectacular walk round Wiltshire by the eight hundred boys and fifty beaks from my old school, Marlborough. Cheshire was away at the time, and he asked me to accept the cheque from John Dancy, the Master, on his behalf. I shall always remember my astonishment on opening the envelope in front of the eight hundred boys and some of the parents, who no doubt had sponsored their sons for so much a mile, to find the cheque was for £15,000. Hampden Inskip is now in charge of developments in this field.

Even in the days of the "small business" the Trustees had come to feel that the twelve, as they were for a long time, were too many for the efficient despatch of business at their monthly meetings, so they delegated all financial and some administrative work to a Finance and General Purposes Committee. Now that there are twenty-five Trustees the consultants have recommended the conversion of this committee to the status of a full-blooded Executive Committee to consist of six Trustees and the Chairmen of the Standing Committees—Homes Planning, Counselling, Mental Care, Personnel, Publicity and Public Relations and the Family Support Service. So this body has superseded the Finance and General Purposes Committee of the old days and the full body of

Trustees will in future meet quarterly to consider policy in the broadest sense.

I was lucky enough to be invited to one of their early working lunches in Market Mews. It was presided over by Mr. Reid-Herrick, a retired industrialist; it started at one o'clock sharp and was over by half-past three, having dealt with an agenda which included approving a draft lease on a field and its grazing rights with a farmer in Norfolk on behalf of the Grove, the home we visited near Norwich in Chapter One. Other items were a problem raised by the Editor of *The Cheshire Smile*, the house magazine; an interest-free loan to Arnold House at Enfield; salary scales for professional staff; and fund raising. At half-past three most of the Trustees went back to their own jobs. The previous afternoon I had attended the quarterly meeting of the Overseas Committee presided over by Henry Marking, probably an even more prolific globe-trotter than Cheshire himself. For many years this Committee's secretary was the much-loved Maggie Toner, who died in 1979. She was known to innumerable men and women from all over the world who were always made welcome in her office at Number Five.

A glance at the agenda of this very international body will show the extraordinary range of activities of the independent Foundations in the different parts of the world where they operate, for which the London-based Overseas Committee provides a base and a link with the parent Foundation.

Ronald Travers, producer many years ago of *The Six Wives of Henry the Eighth*, who then gave up his career with B.B.C. Television to join Cheshire, is now his Deputy and the International Director of the Foundation; he had just returned to London from a trip to Sierra Leone and Nigeria. The committee was asked to confirm his decision, given on the spot, that the disabled children at the Home in Bo in the interior of Sierra Leone should be paid their school fees for the year. Not till recently, as a result of treatment given with funds from the committee, and because of the variety of aids they now have, could any of them get to the school, which was only just across the road, under their own steam.

There was the freighting by air of wheel-chairs all over the world, which is done by Norman Whiteley, a resident of Athol House, the Dulwich Home, himself a member of the committee and attending the meeting in a wheel-chair; there was a request for £4,000 to buy a bus sent in by the Home at Enugu in Eastern Nigeria; and an estimate of the cost of the international conference which is to be held in London in 1981, designated by the United Nations as the year of the disabled; and there was an item which intrigued me, "U.S.A. Rent £1,500".

It appeared that when Cheshire agreed in 1969 that Ron Travers should go on his behalf to America on a reconnaissance, there were not a few who questioned his judgement. How could the richest country in the world need Cheshire Homes? And during the last ten years it has looked often enough as if they were right. Ron has often told me that it would have been easier for him to raise millions of dollars for a five-hundred-bed hospital than thousands of dollars for a small Cheshire Home. Nevertheless, he did succeed in getting together a steering committee in Madison, New Jersey; and it was there that he and the good people of Madison first learned about the formidable obstacles raised by bureaucracy which stand in the way of small amateur homes for the chronic sick. Nothing much seemed to happen for several years, but Ron plodded on with the project, as did the Madison Steering Committee. Suddenly things began to happen. Exxon gave them three acres of valuable land and they made a successful application to the Farmers' Homes Administration for a $900,000 loan which has now been ratified by Congress; there will still be $700,000 to find, £350,000! But they have learned from Cheshire that it pays to get your foot in the door and go ahead without waiting for all the money you need; so they have advertised for tenders from construction firms and plan to open in 1981.

As Cheshire suspected, the key to making headway was to set up a central Foundation in Washington; and this has been done. After a shaky start it now has a paid secretary, Virginia Pfaff, and, as Cheshire himself reported in May 1979, "the appointment has totally transformed the Washington scene".

The cost of being disabled in America is truly frightening. Ralph Hall, administrator of a large rehabilitation unit at Binghampton, New York State, said that long-term stay for disabled people in his hospital in 1977 cost $70 a day. So he is going to start a Cheshire Home at Binghampton, N.Y.

Meanwhile the first Home to be opened in the U.S.A. has begun its work at Gulfport, Mississippi. At a conference held at the White House in May 1977 which was attended by Cheshire, Mrs. Bonnie White, a lady from the deep south, approached him out of the blue and asked him to come to Mississippi to help start a Home. Although this project was looked on with some suspicion, a temporary Home was started in Gulfport early in 1979 in a rented building made available by the parents of a handicapped boy. In his report to the London Trustees, Cheshire wrote: "I can say without hesitation that, although small with just five residents, it must already rank as one of the best within our Foundation. We had what I can only describe as a splendid heart-warming evening."

But this is only the beginning. Bonnie White has negotiated a loan from the Housing and Urban Development Programme to buy two acres of land and build a new Home for twelve residents. By what Cheshire describes as a "happy coincidence" the Miss U.S.A. Beauty Contest had been held in the hotel he was staying in, and the winner, Marie Terese Friel of New York, agreed to carry out the ground-breaking ceremony for the new Home. "This involved," Cheshire reported, "a hundred yard walk along an extremely rough road, and because of her unfamiliarity with a large gold-plated shovel she was given she and I shared the actual dig. She proved to be an exceptionally sincere and interested person." Just before the ceremony Cheshire was given the keys of the city of Gulfport by the Mayor, and the approach road to the site was cut through wasteland and named "Cheshire Avenue".

Over on the other side of the continent, at Santa Cruz in California, a second Home has been opened as a result of the drive of Mrs. Dorothy Nichol, the English wife of a Professor at Santa Cruz University. Ron Travers unveiled the plaque of "The Dorothy Nichol Cheshire Home" on behalf of the founder in 1979; and there are plans for Homes at the Catholic University of Washington and Penn University, Pennsylvania. As so often has been the case with Cheshire throughout his career, I believe there is a long-term plan behind the American venture, that once his formula has been understood and accepted by Americans they will deploy all their native energy and talent for achieving results on a scale that will stagger us all, and they may well take his ideas in the field of care for the disabled further and faster than has been the case in the many lands they have reached already.

It is right, I think, that this book, now brought up to date in this all too abbreviated way, should end with some thoughts of the movement's founder. The evening before the 1979 conference he asked me to go to the small room on the second floor of Number Three, Market Mews. He has such a crowded programme wherever he goes that I would not have been surprised if he had been late. A few minutes before six, the time of the appointment, I heard his voice down in the Mews. And then he was floating through the door without a sound just as he had seemed to me to do on that winter morning in January, 1956, when I first met him carrying a kidney bowl and dressings outside the asbestos cement hut at Santa Cruz in the jungles north of Bombay. He looked fit, although he has been warned by the doctors to cut down on the killing pace of a life devoted all day and every day to the two hundred odd Homes, and for this year he has agreed to a sabbatical of twelve whole months, eroded already to nine.

A good tennis player, he always contrives a game wherever he is. He had come straight from Wimbledon, where he had been playing on clay with the Australian Davis Cup player Ken Fletcher, who won the men's doubles at Wimbledon once with John Newcombe and the mixed doubles four times with Margaret Court. One of the things he treasures a great deal is life membership of Queens, given to him by its committee. His first remark as he sat down was, "Ken's forty now, of course; he generously let me get three games off him!" and then the old grin. As quickly as it had come it was gone and the left palm was up shading the eyes, as he switched on his concentration and quickly marshalled his thoughts.

"Anything new?" I asked.

"I'm writing a book, Wilf, or trying to."

"What about?"

"The reaction of individual people to disability. Hope to finish it next year. There'll be a lot of photographs. I want to try and show what the impact of disability means to the ordinary individual, and half the book will consist of Norman Potter's photographs—he's the best photographer for this kind of subject I know, and has helped enormously." He showed me an album of some of the most striking photographs I have ever seen, of Raphael, the large centre for the severely handicapped and deprived in the foothills of the Himalayas, jointly founded and run by himself and his wife, Sue, now Lady Ryder of Warsaw, a life Peeress.

"I know it sounds obvious, but man really is evolving all the time. What he needs today isn't necessarily what he needed yesterday; and this is particularly true of the disabled. Have you read the report on Staunton?"

I hadn't. I remembered the beautiful Home of the Ferrers family in Leicestershire with its fifty bedrooms which he had saved from demolition back in 1956, so that disabled people who then had nowhere to go were grateful for a bed in a seventeenth-century drawing-room converted into a ward.

"You know Staunton. Today that kind of accommodation just isn't good enough, and the problem there, of course, is how to graft modern single-room accommodation on to that lovely old house. We don't want to have to pull it down after what happened twenty-five years ago." And there was the sudden smile.

He went on, "We simply have to keep up with the times. But are we? I sometimes wonder. People feel that we only react to circumstances and needs, and are not initiators. They are right in a way, and I agree we should now begin to act in anticipation of needs—but only within limits. All our major turning points have been the result of having been confronted with an unexpected situation or human need calling for action. I feel that in this way our course has been plotted for us by Providence."

Then he went on to talk about some of the new experiments which Peter Allott had mentioned—day centres, family support programmes, small Homes attached to larger ones, bungalows for married couples with a disabled partner, built near established Homes for moral and medical support.

"Flexibility, that's what we've got to have, and willingness to listen to criticism. It's so easy to get hidebound and stuck in a groove, especially if you seem to have done rather well in that groove. We really need young people on the committees and among the Trustees. So we have to meet today's needs in today's ways; and it's not as easy as it sounds, especially when you have a place like Staunton Harold with a great hill behind it and a historic church in front with not much room on either end to stick a modern wing, even if the Historic Buildings Council would let us, which they certainly wouldn't, and rightly."

Then, with his gift for seeing the dangers of over-reacting, he explained how important it was not to discard old and well-tried methods just because new ones have come into fashion.

"There's a vocal minority in this country, and an even more vocal one in the United States, which claims that residential Homes for the disabled are out of date, that ideally every disabled person should be able to live in his own home. But I disagree with that if it is meant to apply to all disabled people. As an ideal for those to whom it applies I wholeheartedly support it, but there are so many whose disability is too severe for them ever to manage on their own, and who feel happier and more secure, and will find more self-fulfilment, in a residential Home—assuming it's the right kind of Home. America, for instance, undoubtedly leads the world in independent living and rehabilitation, and has much to teach us on this score. But I feel that this is to a certain extent at the expense of those too disabled ever to manage on their own, or who perhaps don't want to; so many of the younger of them are therefore relegated to nursing homes or long-term care institutions amongst the very old."

He went on: "So there is a continuing demand for residential Homes, but for some people it need only be a temporary one. I've noticed that newcomers to a Home undergo a subtle change after a while. Their horizons broaden, some want to get married, most of them wake up one morning and say to themselves, 'Hi, I want to get out of here,' and that would never have happened if they hadn't come in out of the cold in the first place. By the same token it won't happen if they can't feel that if they do go out into the world again, and should happen to fail, they can return to the Home. Another criticism of our method is that we create ghettos by creating Homes. This is not true if the Home is integrated into its surroundings."

Then he went on to talk about the international scene.

"I'm pretty sure that by now the overseas Foundations do appreciate that our Foundation here in London is not the boss and that they are as independent as we are. I just happen, for the moment, to be Chairman of the International Council because in 1969 they asked me to be."

Then he talked about the doubts some people in the U.K. Foundation had expressed about giving money to Frenchmen and Americans to start up Homes in their countries. I remembered the mysterious item on the agenda of the Overseas Committee—"U.S.A. Rent £1,500". I asked him what it meant.

"Rent for the Washington office. Seed money. Probably the only time we shall have to pay it. The central Council there is going well now and is receiving many requests for information or help for starting Homes from different parts of the country. But to raise money for a central office in the American scene is very difficult. Once they are off the ground not only will the Homes spread across the country, as they have already done in Canada, but America is bound to reach out and help those in the developing countries."

This book has been liberally sprinkled with stories, many of them almost fairy tales except that we know they really did happen. I am going to finish this post-postscript with one that Leonard Cheshire told me in that upper storey room in the mews cottage just before I left him. It had only happened a few months back and it was told, I'm sure, to illustrate that in his mind it is so often the contribution of just one ordinary individual which opens the door that nothing else seems able to move. In Washington, where the British Ambassador and his wife, Sir Peter and Lady Ramsbotham, had originally invited Cheshire and Ron Travers to come and talk about the Homes, the hope of a local Home, once so bright, seemed to be fading altogether, despite an influential and dedicated Board. But Cheshire had an old wartime friend who lived there.

It had all started in the last war when people in the R.A.F. who were sent to Washington were put up in the Gralyn Hotel in N. Street, owned and run by a lovely person, Polly Morrison. Cheshire was posted there in 1945. He arrived late at night and was put into a room with several others. He hung his uniform jacket on the bedside chair, and he must have covered it up with a shirt. At any rate his row of medals was not showing. Perhaps this was one of the things that endeared him to her. At all events she had become fond of him from then on, and they had always kept in touch at Christmas. Almost the first thing he did on arriving in Washington to address a Forum on disabled people at the Embassy was to call on Polly Morrison. It was a very moving reunion. He found her a little frail, at the age of eighty or so, but very welcoming and very interested in his plans. She just said, very quietly, "I'll help you." No one on the Board took this very seriously, for without any prospect of a Home in the Washington area there seemed little that she could do. But one day she just made up her own mind and said to the Board, "I have a little house in Arlington, which was used as a small hospital in the Civil War. You can have it if you like."

At the very moment when I bring these lines to a close, the house has received zoning permission for conversion to a Home for eight disabled people, both the Government authorities and the local community have come forward to help, saying such a Home is badly needed, and all in all the stage looks set for a steady expansion in the United States.

As I got up to go Cheshire spoke again: "What was that you said about your impressions after ten years?"

"That a lot has changed, but not the things that really matter."

"I'm glad."